JUSTICE-CENTERED HUMANISM

Humanism in Practice

Series Editor
Anthony B. Pinn
Rice University
Institute for Humanist Studies (Washington, DC)

Humanism in Practice presents books concerned with what humanism says about contemporary issues. Written in a reader-friendly manner, the books in this series challenge readers to reflect on human values and how they impact our current circumstances.

JUSTICE-CENTERED HUMANISM

HOW (AND WHY) TO ENGAGE IN PUBLIC POLICY FOR GOOD

ROY SPECKHARDT

PITCHSTONE PUBLISHING
Durham, North Carolina

and

INSTITUTE FOR HUMANIST STUDIES
Washington, DC

Pitchstone Publishing
Durham, North Carolina
www.pitchstonebooks.com

Institute for Humanist Studies
Washington, DC
www.humaniststudies.org

10 9 8 7 6 5 4 3 2 1

Library of Congress Cataloging-in-Publication Data

Names: Speckhardt, Roy, author.
Title: Justice-centered humanism : how (and why) to engage in public policy
    for good / Roy Speckhardt.
Description: Durham, North Carolina and Washington, DC : Pitchstone
    Publishing and Institute for Humanist Studies, 2020. | Series: Humanism
    in practice | Includes bibliographical references. | Summary: "Argues
    for a humanism that centers social and environmental justice as a core
    principle and calls on humanists to pursue public policy based on this
    principle"— Provided by publisher.
Identifiers: LCCN 2020053322 (print) | LCCN 2020053323 (ebook) | ISBN
    9781634312097 (paperback) | ISBN 9781634312103 (ebook)
Subjects: LCSH: Political planning—Moral and ethical aspects—United
    States. | Political participation—Moral and ethical aspects—United
    States. | Social justice—United States. | Environmental justice—United
    States. | Humanistic ethics.
Classification: LCC JK468.P64 S74 2020 (print) | LCC JK468.P64 (ebook) |
    DDC 172/.20973—dc23
LC record available at https://lccn.loc.gov/2020053322
LC ebook record available at https://lccn.loc.gov/2020053323

For my daughters, Johanna and Max

CONTENTS

* * *

JUSTICE-CENTERED HUMANISM

INTRODUCTION

* * *

Tuesday evening, February 13, 2018, I was exiting Capitol South Metro Station in Southeast Washington, DC, when I heard a familiar voice call, "Hey, Roy!" Turning, I saw Ron Millar, political and political action committee (PAC) coordinator for the Center for Freethought Equality, the politically oriented sister organization to the American Humanist Association (AHA), where I serve as executive director. We were both on our way to a potentially historic meeting at the Capitol Hill townhouse of U.S. Representative Jared Huffman (D-CA).

As Ron and I walked together, we chatted about the years of work that had led to this moment and what might come if it. I asked him if he remembered the early days of the Secular Coalition for America, an advocacy group founded in 2002 for nontheists—those who don't believe in a god or gods. I reminded him that's when we first began to discuss the idea of a congressional caucus, one that would support the rights and values of the secular movement. "I believe it was originally your idea, Ron," I said.

"That may be right. I think I included it in the vision statement that was asked of me when I was hired," he replied. Back then, the prospect of having the critical mass needed to support such a caucus seemed so distant. At that time, not one member of Congress publicly identified as a humanist or nontheist—that is, until 2007, when Rep. Pete Stark (D-CA) became the first active member of Congress to go public about not believing in a god. "That led us to talk more seriously about how a caucus could transform our movement and our relationships on Capitol Hill," Ron added. Caucuses, or

Congressional Member Organizations, as they are called internally, can wield significant power, like that seen with the Congressional Progressive Caucus, the Congressional Black Caucus, and (somewhat ironically) the Congressional Prayer Caucus, which was still relatively new at the time.

I could barely contain my excitement. "This could be the beginning of a group in Congress that represents our movement! We could be about to be part of history!" But that wasn't the only potential outcome. "Of course, it could also just as easily get derailed," I worried. "What's the worst case scenario?"

"Well," Ron responded, "things could go sour, other members of Congress might not show, and this initial meeting might be indefinitely delayed. Or, even worse, others could show but they could all convince each other to stay in the closet about their support for humanists and other freethinkers."

The latter scenario would be especially problematic since Rep. Huffman had only recently come out as a humanist and nontheist, just the second member of Congress in history to do so while in office, and the only one still in office. That was a process itself. Some folks had reached out to Rep. Huffman to explore his theological views or lack thereof, but hadn't heard back. But when Ron sent his typical candidate survey to Huffman, he replied with a completed survey suggesting his religious identity was "unresolved," so Ron set up a meeting between the three of us. When Ron and I met with him in September 2017, he was almost ready to publicly discuss his personal convictions but was concerned that doing so might inadvertently offend his respected religious family and constituents. He also didn't want to inject the religion question into his qualifications for public service, because he didn't think it was very relevant and there shouldn't be religious or nonreligious tests for public office. So I gave him the primer on humanism I wrote, *Creating Change Through Humanism*, and assured him that through humanism, one can be clear about one's progressive nontheistic identity without offending anyone—except, perhaps, those on the far Religious Right. Days later, Huffman said that he had read the book and given it some thought and that he was on board for an announcement. Although it had been a long ten years since Rep.

Stark's announcement, Huffman's went exceedingly well. The publicity he received inside and outside his district was highly positive.

"It's true," I replied, bringing my thoughts back to the present. "That would delay things years into the future. But so long as Huffman remains strong, it's not so terrible really since we'd be right where we are now, without a group in Congress. Really, there's nothing but upside here."

We reached his townhouse, which Rep. Huffman shared with then U.S. Representative Beto O'Rourke (D-TX) and U.S. Representative Salud Carbajal (D-CA), and a few minutes later, Rep. Huffman arrived to let us in. He ordered some pizza, and we helped set his little kitchen table, which included glasses of water as well as wine from his district, and sat as we waited to see if anyone else would show up.

They did, and this humble meeting marked the start of one of the most significant public policy advances for humanists and freethinkers in U.S. history.

Public policy is a complex network of codes, rules, and practices by which much of our society is bound. The strands of its web are the laws, regulations, and decisions by those in government that should be rooted in the structure of our constitution, foundational principles, and an honest effort to achieve the best potential consequences. Inherent in public policy is the understanding that it exists to promote the public good.

Among those who follow a specific philosophical or religious perspective, humanists may be the most naturally suited to engaging in public policy work. Humanists start with an understanding that the scientific method (observation, experimentation, and rational analysis) is the best way to accumulate and evaluate knowledge. Together with the pillars of compassion derived from empathy, and an egalitarian-based sense of fairness, humanists hold to a philosophy of life that, without supernaturalism, affirms our ability and responsibility to lead ethical lives of personal fulfillment that aspire to the greater good. The AHA's well-known motto, "Good Without a God," distills this philosophy to its essence and communicates in the simplest terms the foundation on which humanism rests.

Unlike those bound by an exceptionalist religion that denigrates outsiders, humanists view this world as having one people equally deserving of dignity. Not subscribing to any rosy mythological concepts of life on Earth, we see the climate change we've perpetrated (accidentally or not) upon this planet, and we know that we must work to preserve the environment for the good of ourselves and other life with which we share this world. Not anarchical or spurning society like some, humanists enthusiastically embrace a responsibility for acting to make everything we experience better. The closing lines of "Humanism and Its Aspirations," a document signed by two dozen Nobel Prize winners that further clarifies the core values of humanist philosophy and challenges humanists to take action toward making this world a better place, read, "Thus engaged in the flow of life, we aspire to this vision with the informed conviction that humanity has the ability to progress toward its highest ideals. The responsibility for our lives and the kind of world in which we live is ours and ours alone." Indeed, while our reason-based approach exposes the challenges that exist in life, suffering is not our guidepost. Rather, we wonder at the possibilities before us, delight at discovery, and constantly soak up the meaning imbued in both our individual and shared life experiences.

Starting with these reference points for humanism, a great deal can be discerned about the best public policy direction on nearly every contemplatable issue. Although not always explicitly stated, implicit in humanism's foundational goal of making the world better for ourselves and for others is the pursuit of justice. Unencumbered by dogma or inertia, humanism has a history of being active in or even at the vanguard of movements for equal rights, but rarely have such justice-based pursuits been formally entwined with the very definition and identity of being a humanist. Similarly, people across the humanist and freethought movement readily embrace being "Good Without a God," but they frequently do not define the "good" clearly enough for it to be a guidepost for day-to-day decision-making. This volume seeks to rectify that oversight by using humanist principles and scientific knowledge to arrive at conclusions regarding what the good should be. These conclusions, in turn, are meant to serve as a guide as we work to make the world a more humanistic one.

The first section of this volume begins with an exploration of how public policy is created. Part evolution, part power-broking, part idealism, public policy development is a constant push-me pull-you between many who often see their goals fade into the distance just as others see them ascend into view. Public policy may be the best path to systemic change, but moving the needle on policy isn't easy, and when it happens it's rare that the change is immediate or dramatic. By examining the experience of nontheist lobbying in Washington, DC, I then offer a sense of the kind of progress our movement has experienced to date and the great potential that lies before us today. I also discuss the work of an active politician, specifically, U.S. Representative Jamie Raskin (D-MD), as an example of someone who lives and votes by humanistic principles. Raskin is part of a new breed of high-integrity humanist politicians who are already making an impact. Once they reach critical mass, they will be a major force behind a future wave of humanistic policy changes. I conclude the section by considering how humanists might think about their relationship to some of the more "charged" issues of public life. It takes effort to best determine what we aim to do with public policy and define whom we seek to benefit. Examining how we can focus our attention on applying humanist principles helps us generalize what humanists "should" do (and not do) in relationship to public policy.

Section two begins with a review of humanism's intersectional approach to social justice and offers specific justice-centered policy recommendations for those issues that relate to race, gender, the LGBTQ community, and the environment.

Section three considers how best to uphold Jefferson's wall of church-state separation and ensure fair secular governance. It also outlines the political edges of humanism and examines, specifically, how humanists should address conservatism. Can one be conservative and a humanist at the same time? Are there problems with trying to be socially liberal and fiscally conservative? While many humanists would disagree on these matters, this discussion aims to challenge our thinking. Finally, I present what I believe to be the true foundation of good public policy—philosophically, consequentially, effectively—and argue how best to balance short-term aims with long-term goals.

Good public policy affects everyday Americans for the better and creates a culture of egalitarianism.

Once the pieces of this puzzle are viewed together, one can see more than ever that being the best humanists we can be entails a number of responsibilities. We should endeavor to rely only upon knowledge based on reason and evidence. We should seek positive consequences for ourselves and society that reflect empathy, compassion, and egalitarianism. Finally, we must realize that the path to achieving a better world cannot be limited to our own experiences, which do not exist in a vacuum, and must commit to an integrated search for justice and happiness for all.

SECTION I
HUMANIST-CENTERED PUBLIC POLICY

1

WHY PUBLIC POLICY?

* * *

When Donald Trump shocked much of the world by winning the 2016 U.S. presidential election, the endless questioning began among progressives: how could such an injustice have occurred? To be sure, the election was exceedingly close. Trump won the electoral vote but lost the popular vote by more than twice as many votes as any previously elected president in U.S. history.

Just considering how close the final tally was, any number of causes could have tipped the scales the other way and resulted in Hillary Clinton being the first woman elected president of the United States. Many charged that Trump had colluded with Russia to help secure victory. But the truth is, with or without foreign interference, Trump rode a growing wave of regressive populist attitudes that had been propelling other politicians on the right—often the far right—to victory around the globe.

A few months earlier, in the United Kingdom, concerns about immigration, economic instability, and terrorism—all magnified by a politicized media bent on using fear to attract viewers and readers—led a majority of Brits to vote in favor of leaving the European Union in the Brexit referendum. Across the English Channel, meanwhile, multiple European countries faced a rise in right-wing extremism. Elsewhere in the world, Brazil and the Philippines elected far-right populist leaders, the pro-Hindu government in India continued to mobilize support for its nationalist agenda, and the ruling Islamist-oriented party in Turkey won a referendum that significantly increased the powers of the country's president.

U.S. Senator Elizabeth Warren (D-MA) pointed out that Trump had capitalized on a "stew of racism" that he actively stirred—for example, by blaming the nation's problems on, as Warren put it, "Those people who don't worship like you, those people who don't look like you, those people who aren't the same color as you." Indeed, it seemed apparent to many that Trump enabled supporters to openly express racist and xenophobic ideas that had long existed but that had not been so readily articulated in public in recent years. These expressions of bigotry weren't limited to questions of race or national origin.

Prior to 2016, many underestimated the level of unbridled misogyny in America. But it was certainly on display during the presidential election as people unfairly critiqued Hillary Clinton not only regarding her qualifications but also for failings that were common among past presidents and even more prevalent in her opponent. As Lauren Besser, a national organizer for the 2017 Women's March on Washington, asked in a *Huffington Post* article, "When does political experience, public service, and international expertise become a liability for our highest public office in the land?" Her answer: when those qualities are held by a woman. The misogyny in our culture is so deeply ingrained that many American women themselves accepted sexist attacks against Clinton.

It seemed that the dumbing down of the United States was at its height when George W. Bush was elected president over Al Gore and proceeded to make decisions based on his religiously imbued gut feelings rather than on hard evidence. Liked by some voters because of his drinking-buddy demeanor, Bush frequently advertised his own ignorance, such as when he said in August 2004, "Our enemies are innovative and resourceful, and so are we. They never stop thinking about new ways to harm our country and our people, and neither do we." But the Trump era changed the game by bringing new lows of ignorance, bigotry, and disrespect for modern knowledge to our nation's top office.

Despite the *New York Times* naming him the least factually accurate candidate, he won the 2016 election. And despite his continuing efforts to mislead, Trump administration lies were often accepted as truth. Perhaps this was due to a conglomeration of right-wing news sources like Fox News and Breitbart, which place their political ends over accurate reporting, ushering in a new era of fake news. Perhaps it was due to a concerted effort by those who sought to gain from U.S. politics, like the Russians who manipulated social media networks to bolster Trump's chances at the presidency, which helped drive cultural degradation.

Looking back on the 2016 election, Trump's "drain the swamp" chant did so well because people see Congress as an almost-never changing body of self-interested elites who retain their positions despite everyday people losing their jobs or being underemployed due to working part-time and losing wages. People were frustrated because they felt they lacked a meaningful voice in the political system. This was especially true in rural America where the middle class was particularly feeling a financial crunch. It helped drive an antiestablishment sentiment. Although they saw Trump as a maverick political outsider, he was actually a so-called one-percenter who had been enmeshed with politicians, celebrities, and the mega-rich his whole life, far from the outsider he painted himself as being.

Recognizing this sad state of affairs, with leaders and media personalities manipulating a misinformed public to support their personal agendas, the challenge could not look much more daunting. But just as with the global environment, the political struggles faced in the United States and elsewhere are in our hands to address, no matter the administration in power. These factors speak to the need of humanists to get more active in public policy, but how do we know that public policy is the realm in which we have hope for progress?

Helping Individuals or Helping the World?

When I considered my career options in college, I knew I wanted to make the world a better place, but I wasn't sure about the best way to go about it. There are so many options for public service within education, charity, advocacy, politics, government, and more.

My first interest was a career in teaching. Doing good on your own is great, but over the course of a career in teaching, you have an opportunity to inspire a veritable army to go out there and pursue change. It's hard to argue with the merits of this strategy, but after a time I realized that I had too little patience and too much of a hands-on orientation to only teach others who might eventually one day see the effects of their own efforts. Of course, I don't want to suggest that teaching's only value rests in some distant future impact. Teachers can have an immediate and direct positive impact on students, the kind of person-to-person improvement that goes hand-in-hand with similar targeted service efforts such as social work, addiction recovery, and food programs, which together do much to alleviate specific difficulties individuals face. Many people I knew who were similarly motivated to better the world pursued careers that allowed them such face-to-face interaction.

Direct charitable efforts are undeniably good. Feeding the hungry, housing the homeless, providing legal aid, and giving medical care all help millions. But I was always struck by how imperfect such efforts must necessarily be. Too many fall through the cracks, drop out, go hungry, freeze on the streets, get treated unjustly, fail to get needed medicine, and experience other tragedies. Not only do existing government programs and direct charities cast an unfortunately porous net, but they also rarely focus on underlying circumstances that give rise to the problems that call out for their help and attention. While humans may be hardwired to feel more compassion for individuals as opposed to groups, such limitations are surmountable through choice and experience.

Direct charity certainly makes things better for the individuals it serves as long as it is serving them, but such efforts are stop-gap measures that are never-ending if nothing is done to prevent people from getting down on their luck in the first place. In fact, alleviating the problems of individuals could actually slow systemic change by preventing individual strife from reaching levels that draw appropriate attention to the problems—often such attention is needed to gain the necessary public support and spur officials to devise and implement longer-lasting solutions. Unless direct charity incorporates social change measures or their work goes side-by-side with advocacy efforts, they may actually perpetuate cultural norms rather than push to shift them.

In 2016 Doctors Without Borders (Médecins Sans Frontières) rejected a million free vaccines from Pfizer that would have inoculated against a life-threatening type of pneumonia. Doctors Without Borders rejected the donation as an insufficient solution to the problem of the vaccine's prohibitively high price that was preventing them, and other charities, from inoculating millions more. In so doing, Doctors Without Borders chose public policy advocacy over short-term charity in hopes of helping more people over the long term.

Some charities mix their advocacy with their charity like Doctors Without Borders, and some charitable work inherently sows the seeds of change. SMART Recovery, which helps individuals abstain from addictions, doesn't teach people to give over their autonomy to a higher power, unlike Alcoholics Anonymous. Instead, SMART Recovery uses scientifically based rational emotive therapy to help people gain control over their own lives. Through that example, SMART Recovery shows people they can make positive change in the world around them. Big Brothers Big Sisters doesn't just provide resources to poor kids; it also adds mentorship and exposes kids to enough of the world that they can discover the lack of fairness of their circumstances, potentially inspiring them to seek social change. Further, the big brothers and big sisters who participate in the program may be inspired toward further humanistic pursuits when they see just how much privation is endured outside their own immediate circles. Even those in traditional professions, such as counselors, can be change agents by being situated to identify injustices and ally with others to expose them. But even considering great options like these that make real and lasting differences, I couldn't help wanting to be involved in something that would enable me to more readily see the broad change that I hoped to effect.

Upon further consideration, I was more attracted to efforts specifically designed to result in systematic change as opposed to those that do so inadvertently or tangentially. Broadly speaking, there are two approaches to this. One is working within the system in traditional public policy advocacy—that is the focus of this book. The other is working outside the system, such as by promoting communism, libertarianism, or some other revolutionary departure from our current political and economic structure. Radical departures from the status quo need not require rebellion, physical or otherwise, but the required power shifts inevitably lead to some destabilization just as any abrupt shift in power destabilizes economies and practices for a time.

There's certainly something to be said for radical approaches. After all, those with power in government and business are not going to cede that power without a struggle. Such struggles have led to setbacks in the advance of true democracy, as best exemplified in the *Citizens United v. Federal Election Commission* decision—the 2010 Supreme Court ruling that essentially provided corporations the same rights as citizens, giving them more power than ever to influence politics in their favor. While some progressive politicians promise to work toward overturning this ruling and putting power back in the hands of the people, it's a fair question as to whether this can really happen within the system.

Similarly, there are other societal challenges that seem so overwhelming in their pervasiveness that conventional approaches seem to delay the possibility of change unacceptably far into the future. An example of this is seen in our criminal justice system, which has targeted Black Americans for centuries. As I'll explore in chapter 6, this raises the question, can traditional approaches using the political process hope to succeed in correcting highly entrenched wrongs?

The somewhat daunting recognition of just how far we have to go suggests to some that the only real solutions may be outside the system, like forming a new political party, building an independent commune or kibbutz, or leaving the United States for another country. Sometimes change requires good people to challenge the law, such as the doctors that helped women seek abortions where and when it was illegal. Organizations like Women on Waves do what it takes to ensure women have reproductive rights, just as groups like the Final Exit Network help those seeking death with dignity. There's no doubt that such options are needed today, but wouldn't it be great if we could have the society we want without consistently challenging the rule of law or escaping to another country?

A fair retort to those seeking revolutionary change is that their approach is even less realistic than gradual political change. After all, truly revolutionary efforts may lie outside First Amendment protected rights. That not only opens up the individuals involved to risk of legal action and government-sponsored violence but also threatens their radical aims in other key ways.

By going outside the system, a target of sorts is painted on the cause, inviting government and other power brokers to counter any productive efforts. I see this in modest ways when the far right successfully fundraises and mobilizes its members by painting mainstream and left-leaning folks as part of a radical left-wing conspiracy to overturn society. And I see it in more direct ways as well. It's now well documented, as evidenced in the work of Zaheer Ali, former project manager of the Malcolm X Project at Columbia University, that the government infiltrated Malcolm X's Organization of Afro-American Unity, as happened to a number of organizations that challenged the existing system—including the American Humanist Association.

One of the American Humanist Association's biggest historic investors, past president and past *Humanist* magazine editor Lloyd Morain, relayed to me his own experience of governmental intrusion at the organization. Morain told me how the American Humanist Association was contacted in the 1960s by two people who looked like federal agents, complete with crew cuts, dark suits, and secretive manner. They said they wanted to research humanism and better understand the organization. Understanding what they were likely after, and choosing not to protest, the organization's leadership responded by opening the doors for them and inviting them to research our files, attend local group meetings, and get to know the humanist movement. During their roughly six months of attending meetings and reviewing our materials and correspondence, they never acknowledged that they were working for the government. The closest they came was at the end of their "study," when their leader confided to then AHA director Ed Wilson that he came looking to bust us, to prove that we were a threat to national security, but that in the end he decided we weren't a threat. He also actually realized that he was a humanist himself! Later, through multiple Freedom of Information Act (FOIA) requests, it was confirmed that they were indeed agents of the Federal Bureau of Investigation (FBI) assigned to investigate whether or not the AHA was a threat. Other than noting some known communists who attended our meetings at the time, the agents' notes concluded that we were not an imminent threat. That's fortunate, because had they determined the AHA to be a threat, they might have made it impossible for us to continue operations and seek the changes to public policy that we now seek today.

The other problem with seeking immediate radical change is that such aims are viewed by the majority as extreme political positions. Whether communism, libertarianism, or anarchical redistributions, such variances from our democratic system are commonly viewed as the musings of dreamers who are out of touch with the real world. Those who seek to market their ideas find greater success when positioning them as a mainstream struggle for universal principles. Fortunately, as great a departure humanism is from present politics, it is undergirded by foundational American principles, and taken individually, most humanist viewpoints receive popular support or at the very least the support of large minorities of the population. Humanist visions are achievable short of revolution.

Leveraging Politics to Make Change

This path brings us to politics. Whether we're aiming to be one of the few elected officials or the many who aim to influence those officials, it's all the realm of public policy.

For me, a career in electoral politics wasn't where I thought I could make the biggest difference. Part of that stemmed from my experience at the Interfaith Alliance in the 1990s. The organization was formed when politically connected people realized that the Christian Coalition and other organizations on the Religious Right were walking all over the left in accomplishing their socially conservative agendas. The politicos organizing the Interfaith Alliance were convinced that a strong religious left could effectively counter the Religious

Right's regressive campaigns. That strategy did see some significant success.

During the Christian Coalition's height it distributed millions of voter guides in churches across the country that not so subtly supported the ultraconservative religious candidates. Such biased voter guides had a real impact on campaigns, and the wealthy on the far right would jump at the chance to fund the Christian Coalition with tax-deductible dollars in order to see more of their cronies get elected. One of the Interfaith Alliance's most effective campaigns was sending well-designed letters to thousands of clergy signed by fellow clergy they might respect, warning them against distributing the Christian Coalition's biased voter guides. These letters worked wonders, resulting in massive numbers of Christian Coalition voter guides going undistributed—undoubtedly also impacting elections.

One day in the spring of 1996, I joined the organization's founding executive director, Jill Hanauer, to visit those who might be able to help us secure funding to expand our warning-letter campaigns against the voting guide. Our meeting was at the AFL-CIO headquarters building, just steps from the White House. As Hanauer waited her turn to speak to those assembled, we caught the tail-end of an interesting conversation. Representatives of the Democratic National Committee (DNC) were being bluntly told by AFL-CIO leadership that the campaign advertisement they were running was unacceptable and must be pulled and replaced that very day. Far from challenging the demand, or pointing out the impropriety of a labor union calling the shots on electoral activity, the DNC representative meekly agreed to do what was asked.

When it was her turn, Hanauer gave a strong appeal for the support of our campaign. While I don't recall her offering anything legally inappropriate, the questions asked of her seemed to cross lines. They wanted to know if the voting guide warning letters could be targeted to specific states and political districts. They wanted to be able to control that targeting so that the letters would have an impact on existing campaigns. As effective as the Interfaith Alliance was, this experience was eye-opening.

Seeing this first-hand had its plusses and minuses. It helped brush off some of my naive idealism and helped me see just how powerful advocacy organizations can be when they are influencing the process. Combined with other news about the electoral process, it made me a bit jaded about those in elected office and what it takes to get such a position. I wasn't willing to compromise as much as seemed necessary to be successful in such an arena, so I wrote off the idea of electoral politics for some time—not just for me personally, but even as something with which to be closely associated.

Fortunately, I've rediscovered the positive potential electoral politics holds, and that was rekindled by the examples of others. While we've had other impressive principled politicians like Paul Wellstone in the past and Elizabeth Warren in the present, it was humanist Jamie Raskin's incredible accomplishments as a Maryland state senator (described in chapter 2) that made me realize that politicians themselves can be true forces for change.

Now knowing that potential exists, I'm pleased that the American Humanist Association has a sister lobbying organization, the Center for Freethought Equality, with its own political action committee, the Freethought Equality Fund PAC. This political action committee supports humanists and freethought candidates for public office as well as religiously minded candidates who agree to support nontheist rights and religion-government separation. Having the first sustainable PAC in the humanist and atheist movement has opened doors and increased the interest of many politicians in listening to our perspective, making our lobbying and advocacy efforts much more effective. One might surmise that this is for unsavory reasons—a case of politicians willing to do anything for an extra few dollars for their campaign—but there's another view of this as well. Sometimes politicians simply see a cause with a PAC as being more sophisticated than a cause without one. And it's not just sophistication, because an active PAC demonstrates the ability of the organization to "have the back" of the politician. Politicians are understandably more willing to go out on a limb for an organization's cause when that same organization can provide positive public relations support to them.

When we were seeking sponsors for our National Day of Reason resolution in 2016, the staff of U.S. Representative Mike Honda (D-

CA) communicated an initial reluctance to sponsor it, even though Matthew Bulger, AHA's legislative director, had convinced them to sponsor the same bill the previous year. When our PAC manager, Bishop McNeil, reached out to his office, Rep. Honda agreed to set aside time to meet personally with us. It was a fascinating meeting. Rep. Honda spent at least half an hour describing his personal experiences with faith and how he became somewhat disenchanted with organized religion. During that meeting he expressed how he was all too happy to continue to sponsor the National Day of Reason resolution.

Despite my broadening perspective on the effectiveness of other paths to activism and societal change, I'm still convinced public policy advocacy is the best way to challenge societal norms, push for changes in law, and persuade powers like government to change course in a way that makes our society better for everyone. Public policy advocacy best leverages dollars and time by focusing on activism that can move policy and change the minds of enough people so that real transformation is unstoppable. Though it may be the best path to change that can impact the whole nation and beyond, in practice, rapid change through such methods is rare, so one has to focus rather narrowly in order to see it happening. Even then policies regularly go forward and backward as leadership changes and momentum ebbs and flows.

Consider the efforts to prevent guns from being readily accessible to those who might use them to harm others. After nearly every mass shooting there's a surge of support for measures like removing gunshow loopholes that prevent mandatory background checks and registrations from being a reliable system for tracking dangerous weapons. But as strong as the interest of those following the story is, predictably, months later, only those directly affected are asking why legislatures have moved on to other topics, often without getting anything done.

Look at the back-and-forth struggle on reproductive choice. Many thought the battle was won when the Supreme Court handed down *Roe v. Wade* and declared that the Fourteenth Amendment right to privacy extended to a women's ability to decide to have an abortion. But no sooner was the right established than the chipping away at that right began. Just weeks after the Court's decision, the National Right to Life Committee officially formed, and within two years they managed to get a number of abortion providers sued for performing abortions.

Since then, strides were made to make abortions more readily available and Planned Parenthood became the single-largest provider of abortions nationwide. But the 2015 shooting at a Planned Parenthood clinic in Colorado Springs shows that right-wing fear tactics are still provoking violence and hate. Several conservative states are also passing measures aimed at making access to safe abortions more difficult for women. Measures passed in half of the states have led to numerous abortion clinics closing down. With the present composition of the Supreme Court, much of the progress over the last fifty years hangs in the balance.

At the AHA's Humanist Legal Society inaugural event, "The Supreme Court After Kennedy," Maya Rupert, policy director of the Center for Reproductive Rights, said that while the Religious Right ultimately seeks to overturn *Roe v. Wade*, "a panoply of rights around *Roe* will be their first target." She also pointed out how seven states now have only one abortion provider, and eight states ban the standard late-term dilation and extraction (D&E) procedure.

Perhaps one of the most persistently resurging problems relates to campaign finance reform. As soon as progressive-minded activists gain any worthwhile changes, new loopholes are discovered and business as usual resumes, creating an endless game of Whack-a-Mole. When the Bipartisan Campaign Finance Reform Act of 2002 was enacted, for example, it seemed there would be real limits on "soft money," the money that goes to political parties instead of being directed to specific campaigns. The legislation appeared poised to prevent campaign expenditures beyond federal limits and end electioneering ads by nonprofits. However, in *Citizens United*, the Supreme Court ruled that the government cannot prevent corporations from raising money for candidates, and it removed fundraising restrictions placed on political action committees. The result was staggering increases in funds raised and spent. The 2008 presidential campaign, which topped $5.3 billion according the *Wall Street Journal*, was the highest on record, and as organizations continued to take advantage of the new rules, this figure more than doubled in the 2016 campaign. A 2014 measure to overturn *Citizens United* was introduced to the Senate and was approved by every Democrat, but Republican opposition led to the measure failing to pass, as it did not garner the 67 percent needed. Republicans like U.S. Senator Mitch McConnell (R-KY) argued that Democrats were trying to limit the free speech of Americans, but, according to Ramsey Cox's reporting for *The Hill*, the real result was that corporations could influence elections on a much larger scale than any single American could.

As if the existing campaign finance loopholes aren't large enough, some religious conservatives are pushing to do away with the prohibition on churches getting involved in electoral politics. If that happens, considering that funds donated to churches are anonymous, tax-deductible, and unlimited, churches would quickly become the funnel of choice for electioneering money. A likely side-effect of all this money flowing through churches would be significantly increased clout for the larger favored religions, and undoubtedly a further dismantling of the wall of church-state separation.

If making public policy gains appears to be a constant struggle, whereby gains can be lost if positions aren't vigorously defended, then I'm adequately communicating the reality of the challenge. Even so, there are other difficulties to overcome in public policy work.

When considering matters of public policy, the emphasis should be "consequentialist," meaning, in an ideal world, the researchers, influencers, and decision-makers would all consider the consequences of every public policy question on not only individuals but also our society, country, and even world. Decision-making would really be the art of seeing all these factors as they are and balancing them to yield the best result. But realistically, there are many competing interests. Perhaps most important to consider is the ways personal interest can influence the thinking of our public policy decision-makers.

Protecting Their Own

Even though public policy is supposed to be for the common good, there's little to prevent decision-makers from placing their own interests above others, and dismaying examples abound. When it became apparent that presidential candidate Donald Trump had paid little—or perhaps even no—personal income taxes, he explained that he was just being smart. In that context, it wasn't hard to see that Trump's proposed tax cuts for the wealthy were part of that same self-interest, not a considered strategy to benefit everyone. Similarly, Congress has exploited legal loopholes to allow them to learn inside information on businesses and use that to make money in the stock market. What would be illegal insider trading to anyone else is protected to a degree for them, with no obvious benefit to anyone else.

Self-interest that gets in the way of societal benefit isn't always about the individual either; it can be trying to support one's group. That group support can be as small as a set of family and friends, an extended network of neighbors and fellow townspeople, constituents in a political district, residents of a state, or even citizens of a country. In each case, putting the group interest over society's may result in bad public policy. This is commonly seen when members of Congress seek budget allocations for projects that benefit their individual districts—commonly called pork-barrel politics. For example, a member of Congress might seek funding for an airplane manufacturer knowing full well that it would have a special benefit to their district where a Lockheed Martin assembly plant happened to be based. According to the *Department of Defense News*, this practice got so flagrant that in 2016 Defense Secretary Ash Carter sent a letter to Congress telling its members to stop specifying funding for equipment the Pentagon doesn't need and didn't ask for.

It's not just Congress that can get caught up in overprotecting their group interest; advocacy groups can be prone to this as well. Patient advocacy groups, for example, while powerful lobbyists on Capitol Hill, have been surprisingly silent on the debate regarding the overpricing of medicine. But it's not so surprising when one considers that these same groups receive millions of dollars in donations from pharmaceutical companies. Going against the grain on this, as did

Cyndi Zagieboylo, chief executive of the National Multiple Sclerosis Society, in challenging high-priced drugs, is a risky step organizationally, even if it's the moral choice and what's ultimately best for the public good. Similar struggles exist in the movement to keep church and state separate. The American Humanist Association continues to lobby for the right of unaffiliated atheists to perform weddings and against parsonage allowances for clergy on principle, even though this would limit the financial benefits of legally certified nontheist clergy like Humanist Celebrants. Not all groups in the humanist movement have taken this stand, but ideally, advocacy groups should rise above self-interest and seek the best course for society.

Faith-Based Justifications

Of course, spiritually minded policymakers may attempt to ground their thoughts in the shifting sands of faith. By relying on religious faith, which presupposes a lack of evidence, the potential for wrong conclusions is magnified. Faith often rests on books that were written in an ancient age when far less was known about our environment and how the world works, and even less was known about humanity and how we came to exist. An individual's faith is often open to manipulation by charismatic leaders who convey explanations and instructions that conveniently comport with their own interests. Because faith isn't based on testable knowledge, the use of faith as a justification is often a discussion ender, for it is frequently impossible to prove or disprove the accuracy of faith claims.

One of the United States' greatest blunders in recent decades, now acknowledged by many members of the major political parties, was the decision to order an invasion of Iraq in 2003. While those in the George W. Bush administration claimed it was for the public good in order to forestall an imminent threat and prevent the development of so-called weapons of mass destruction, not everyone believed that was true. Some felt it was a Dick Cheney–led self-interest campaign to make money for himself and his buddies through the extraction of oil and the expenditure on consultants like Haliburton, which, according to the *International Business Times*, made $39.5 billion on the

Iraq War. Others argue the war was really juat part of a neoconservative-led crusade to spread Western-style democracy throughout the Middle East, which, if true, was incredibly short-sighted in terms of anticipatable negative consequences.

The commander-in-chief gave another reason for the war: his religious convictions. According to the Israeli newspaper *Haaretz,* when George W. Bush spoke in 2003 to Palestinian Prime Minister Mahmoud Abbas, he said, "God told me to strike at al-Qaida and I struck them, and then he instructed me to strike at Saddam, which I did, and now I am determined to solve the problem in the Middle East. If this is a religious war—a 'clash of civilizations,' waged by competing agents of God's will—victory may be indistinguishable from Armageddon. God help the human race." Not only is this decision an example of bad public policy, but it's also an example of immoral behavior to the extreme.

More recently, conservative Republicans attempted to pass a water and energy budget bill that would address a wide area of issues they favored, such as curtailing clean-water regulations and increasing the places people could carry guns. But when Democrats and moderate Republicans agreed to add a provision barring federal contractors from discrimination based on sexual orientation and gender identity, the rest of the Republicans gave up on the bill rather than offer this basic employment protection to LGBTQ people. As reported by Jennifer Bendery for the *Huffington Post,* "Rep. Rick Allen (R-GA) read aloud a passage from the Bible and asked people if they were prepared to violate their religious principles by supporting the bill." It's a revealing example of how line-in-the-sand religious prejudices can impact the course of public policy discussions.

As Secular Coalition for America founder Herb Silverman has written about how politicians often cherrypick scripture to suit their 'moral' positions: "If a politician focuses on portions of ancient religious texts to justify a vote, I think the politician either has no rational argument for it or is pandering to voters of that faith." Silverman isn't alone in this sentiment. We all see past their pious statements and recognize not only how poor an argument faith-based reasoning is, but also how it's often morally inferior since it frequently suggests supporting only those of like mind—and not the common good of all theists and nontheists.

Public policy is the most effective change agent we have, even with all its failings and potentials for manipulation. The best way to overcome personal, organizational, and religious agendas is to expose them. Exposing all the weaknesses of opposing points of view is an essential part of the arguments we make as humanists, along with the evidence we muster, the appeal to people's compassion we make, and the fairness and positive consequences our recommended approaches demonstrate.

* * *

Recommended Reading

William Cunningham, C. Daryl Cameron, and Michael Inzlicht, "Does Empathy Have Limits? Depends on Whom You Ask," *Conversation,* March 1, 2017. theconversation.com/does-empathy-have-limits-depends-on-whom-you-ask-72637

James Hamblin, "Why Doctors Without Borders Refused a Million Free Vaccines," *Atlantic,* October 14, 2016. www.theatlantic.com/health/archive/2016/10/doctors-with-borders/503786/

Luke Harding, *Collusion: Secret Meetings, Dirty Money, and How Russia Helped Donald Trump Win* (Vintage Press, 2017).

Danielle Kurtzleben, "How to Win the Presidency with 23 Percent of the Popular Vote," *National Public Radio,* November 2, 2016. www.npr.org/2016/11/02/500112248/how-to-win-the-presidency-with-27-percent-of-the-popular-vote

Nipunika O. Lecamwasam, "Iraq Invasion: A "Just War" or Just a War?" University of Colombo, January 2013. www.e-ir.info/2013/06/06/iraq-invasion-a-just-war-or-just-a-war/

Karoline Postel-Vinay, "How Neo-Nationalism Went Global," *U.S. News and World Report,* March 15, 2017. www.usnews.com/news/best-countries/articles/2017-03-15/a-look-at-global-neo-nationalism-after-brexit-and-donald-trumps-election

Herb Silverman, "Vice President of Religion," *OnFaith.com*, October 6, 2016. www.richarddawkins.net/2016/10/vice-president-of-religion/

Rebecca L. Toporek, Judith A. Lewis, and Hugh C. Crethar, "Promoting Systemic Change Through the ACA Advocacy Competencies," *Journal of Counseling & Development* 87 (Summer 2009). www.uwyo.edu/education/_files/documents/diversity-articles/toporek_2009.pdf

2

LOBBYING CONGRESS AND THE WHITE HOUSE

* * *

Compared to some other movements, organized humanists and atheists don't have a lengthy and robust lobbying history, but we have made remarkable progress in the last decade. Historically, humanists were involved with the formation of organizations like the National Association for the Advancement of Colored People, Humanists International, and NARAL Pro-Choice America, but lobbying did not become a priority for humanist organizations until this century. The closest previous attempt at such an effort was during the 1970s when the Joint Washington Office for Social Concern represented the American Humanist Association, the American Ethical Union, and the Unitarian Universalist Association on Capitol Hill.

To my knowledge, I was the first full-time staff person in decades to walk the halls of Congress lobbying on behalf of humanists when I coalesced with others to stop the 2003 Federal Marriage Amendment. That was the bill that, if passed, would have read: "Marriage in the United States shall consist only of the union of a man and a woman. Neither this Constitution or the constitution of any State, nor state or federal law, shall be construed to require that marital status or the legal incidents thereof be conferred upon unmarried couples or groups."

During this campaign I made many calls to congressional offices. I found that engaging in conversations with legislative assistants enabled me to remind liberal representatives to stand up for what's right and to encourage conservative representatives to allow such decisions to be made at the state level. Such arguments were effective; appealing to the values of these leaders and their staffs helped them to see the problems with what would have been the first constitutional amendment restricting rights since liquor prohibition more than eighty years earlier. Working in such a way, we defeated the Federal Marriage Amendment.

It was exciting to be part of an effort that called on Democrats and Republicans alike to hold to their principles. But their willingness to listen and discuss this issue with me was partially based on a false understanding; most Hill staffers weren't aware that humanists don't pray to an intervening god, and I wasn't initially forthcoming in sharing that information with these presumably religious folks. Being a relative newbie to the lobbying scene, I had followed the precedent of past humanist volunteers who worked with groups like the Religious Coalition for Reproductive Choice and the Coalition Against Religious Discrimination, quietly supporting coalition aims without making a fuss about faith-based language they might employ or even opening prayers at coalition meetings.

Over time I spoke more openly with religious lobbying colleagues about the humanist philosophy, and when I became executive director of the American Humanist Association in 2005, I made our organization's position clearer than ever, shedding our previously religiously purposed tax exemption and modifying our public comments so we didn't imply that we believed something we did not. While we were happy to work as allies to groups like the Religious Coalition for Reproductive Choice, we wouldn't be a member or sign on to anything that self-referenced us as "faith leaders," "prayerful," or "understanding our rights are derived from God." Perhaps because we already had built a decent reputation in the federal lobbying community, or perhaps because of the rising boats of all nontheists at the time, this shift didn't negatively impact our reception or our lobbying effectiveness.

In fact, more and more staff on the Hill secretly confided in me that not only were they sympathetic to our viewpoints, but also that they were themselves humanists or nontheists too! And it wasn't an anomaly when one chief of staff to a Virginia senator confessed to me that they suspected their boss was a humanist as well! It takes being open about your humanist ideas to find out who shares your thinking. Once others are aware they are in safe company they are often very willing to be open about their real convictions.

It was also 2005 when the Secular Coalition for America (SCA) hired its first full-time lobbyist in former Nevada State Senator Lori Lipman Brown. Formed in 2002, the SCA was a project of the many movement groups designed to up the ante on what could be accomplished on our behalf in terms of legislative advocacy. The SCA operates as a coalition that helps member organizations better cooperate. Lipman Brown boldly lobbied on our movement's behalf, handing out brochures and business cards emblazoned with the SCA name and logo, and also (very importantly) with the tagline: "Atheists, Agnostics, Humanists. Americans." Just as I was pleased to see her explain the need for a nonreligious lobbyist on *The O'Reilly Factor* and *The Colbert Report* at the time, I am still pleased to see the SCA's current staff continue the good fight today.

Lobbying is like other types of asks in many ways, like fundraising or asking for a favor. It requires the lobbyist to gauge the personality and interests of the government official being lobbied and then to succinctly present information in a persuasive manner. According to Matthew Bulger, legislative director at the Center for Freethought Equality (CFE), the AHA's sister organization lobbying arm,

> Lobbying can be a bit like going on a first date. You can't help but notice the other person's body language and whether or not they are interested in you and what you have to say. If you're doing a good job presenting your agenda and connecting personally with a government official or their staff, short meetings can end up going on for hours and can cover a variety of topics not just related to the issue your organization is advocating on at the moment. On the other hand, heavily religious and conservative government officials can make it clear to you that they want the

meeting to be as short as possible, and in those circumstances you need to be able to get your message out in a brief, nonconfrontational manner that will leave that government official with a better understanding of who you are and what your community wants, even if they don't personally agree with those goals.

Occasionally, elected officials and their staffs will try and spend less time talking with you about the position you're advocating for when it's something they don't agree with or are on the fence about. When lobbying, be sure to stay focused on the task at hand. With some of our long-term and highly respected elected representatives, it can be easy to be a bit starstruck. They'll notice, and they may use the opportunity to redirect difficult conversations to general politics or personal connections. One time, when a colleague and I visited a member of Congress to make a very challenging request, I noticed that the congressperson put out a bowl of dry cookies the moment we walked in. If we had fallen for the ploy and had immediately started eating them, we'd have been unable to lead with our request and have been stuck with the congressperson directing the conversation. Politicians are often experts at avoiding answering questions, but if you're ready for these kinds of tactics, you'll be better able to get your issues addressed.

Lobbying for Darwin Day Recognition

The Center for Freethought Equality lobbies daily on Capitol Hill. The Center helped write the first bill from the humanist movement ever sponsored in the House—the Darwin Day Resolution, which is designed to recognize the international celebration of Charles Darwin's birthday on February 12. Darwin, by the way, like Thomas Jefferson and others, is one of our deeply flawed heroes who we honor for the good he accomplished, not for his prejudiced views or discriminatory actions. Darwin Day itself was made popular in the United States by AHA member Dr. Robert Stephens and continues to be promoted annually by AHA adjunct the Darwin Day Foundation. Getting Congress to issue such a resolution would raise awareness of

Darwin's positive contributions to humanity, the importance of evolution in science classes, and how the scientific thinking that flowed from the debates on evolution helped spawn the modern humanist movement. The process of accomplishing the resolution's introduction was more straightforward than one might think.

The AHA's development director at the time, Maggie Ardiente, filled in on the lobbying front as we were approaching Darwin Day in 2011. I had the idea of reaching out to Rep. Pete Stark (D-CA), the AHA's 2008 Humanist of the Year and the only open humanist serving in Congress at the time, to see if he would be willing to introduce a House Resolution recognizing February 12 as Darwin Day. I thought it might be a long shot, but Ardiente was willing to try. She called Jeff Hild, Rep. Stark's legislative director at the time, and arranged to meet with him in person. Prepared with a draft resolution, Ardiente talked to Hild one-on-one about the importance of Darwin Day and asked for Rep. Stark's support in issuing a formal resolution. Not only did Hild and Rep. Stark agree to introduce the resolution, but they also helped draft additional, stronger language in support of evolution, even adding an item about climate change which, at the time, was being vigorously debated in Congress.

Rep. Stark introduced House Resolution 81 on the floor of the U.S. House of Representatives on February 9, 2011, stating:

> Charles Darwin is worthy of recognition and honor. His birthday should be a time for us to celebrate the advancement of human knowledge and the achievements of reason and science. It should also be a time for Congress and other elected officials to ensure that children are being taught scientific facts and not religious dogma in our public schools.

While the resolution never left committee and was never voted on, Rep. Stark was pleased with the positive press it received along with hundreds of supportive constituent emails and complimentary comments on his Facebook page. In each following year, the bill was reintroduced and gained more and more cosponsors, and with the help of the Secular Coalition for America, it was sponsored in the

Senate as well in 2015. and the AHA ensured it saw repeated sponsorship in years following.

One might see getting a bill introduced but not passed as a loss, especially year after year. But losing isn't always a problem with legislation. Unlike unsuccessful legal actions that can create bad legal precedent preventing future hearings on the same issue, with legislation one can try, try, and try again, and each time you do, you have a new opportunity to get publicity and educate the general public and decision-makers on your issue. Eventually, if you can build upon past support, your aim can be achieved. Similar to the Darwin Day Resolution, the AHA and CFE have worked to regularly introduce a resolution recognizing the National Day of Reason.

Lobbying for a National Day of Reason

Every year on the first Thursday of May, a peculiar thing happens: the president and government officials across the nation ask all Americans to pray. Not only do they ask us to pray, but they also inform us of the value of prayer. According to President Barack Obama's 2012 National Day of Prayer proclamation, prayer has "always been a part of the American story, and today countless Americans rely on prayer for comfort, direction, and strength." Of course, it's not exactly "countless" since we can count millions of Americans who don't believe in the efficacy of prayer.

This is a particular problem for civic-minded nonreligious Americans. Just like our religious family and friends, we want to participate in community gatherings and political events and be an accepted contributor to the diverse American tapestry. We take issue with efforts to say that the American way is the way that excludes us, especially when those efforts are driven by officials we helped elect.

It's not just the excluded nonreligious quarter raising issues with a nationwide prayer. There are also many people of faith that object to government's intrusion in their private religious practices. After all, we didn't elect our representatives to give us advice on how and when to pray, and some particularly devout people believe that reserving prayer for a single day demeans its importance.

As if it weren't bad enough just as a concept, the National Day of Prayer's execution makes it even worse. This national religious "observance" has been around since the 1950s, when, during the McCarthy era, many Americans took pains to distinguish themselves from atheist communist Russia. That's when Congress and President Harry S Truman mandated this day of prayer to occur every year. It was only relatively recently that it became such a focal point, and credit for that goes to George W. Bush, Shirley Dobson, and the National Day of Prayer Taskforce. They steered the observance in a decidedly conservative direction that encourages mixing church and state. During Bush's reign, there were elaborate prayer breakfasts and ceremonies where religious values were praised.

That's why humanists across the country celebrate the more universal National Day of Reason on the same day as the National Day of Prayer. While each local humanist and atheist group is encouraged to come up with their own events, one of the main points of the day is to do something that makes a positive difference in people's lives. That's why during government-sponsored prayer events, nontheist Americans will invite all to participate in community events, like ReasonFest in Lawrence, Kansas, which helps raise funds for charity, and Gift For Life, a blood donation drive in New York City.

Elected officials like Nebraska Governor David Heinemann, U.S. Representative Eleanor Holmes Norton (D-DC), and U.S. Transportation Secretary Anthony Foxx have all issued statements recognizing the National Day of Reason and calling upon Americans to utilize reason and critical thinking when solving today's problems. U.S. Representative Mike Honda (D-CA) submitted a statement to the Congressional Record honoring the day and reaffirming the "constitutional separation of religion and government."

Lobbying against Religious Intrusion into Government

By aggregating the power and influence of multiple lobbying groups, legislative coalitions account for a very significant proportion of all that happens on Capitol Hill. This is somewhat difficult for noninsiders to see for a number of reasons that mostly revolve around who gets credit for what. As a lobbyist working for an organization your first priority is to achieve your legislative aims, but it's even better if you and your organization can claim credit for doing so. Often, however, credit goes to a coalition that you're part of that really collectively pulled the strings to make things happen. When a progressive bill is passed or a religious conservative initiative is stymied, you might see a news report or even the press releases news reports are based upon, touting the good work of advocacy organizations like the American Civil Liberties Union or People for the American Way. Don't be fooled: in such cases, they definitely had a role in the outcome, but often the real influence is dispersed among a coordinated group. The work of legislative coalitions is thus almost never in the news.

With rare exceptions, legislative coalitions don't hire staff, don't have websites, and don't promote themselves; they just facilitate their members' goals. Many only exist so long as a particular legislative push is active. For instance, there was a time when conservative politicians were seeking to prevent the courts from hearing cases on issues the courts might side with humanists on—like church-state separation issues. They did this by seeking to pass constitutionally questionable legislation colloquially called "court-stripping" bills, which would make it illegal for the courts to even hear such cases. The AHA successfully led a coalition to prevent these court-stripping bills from ever reaching a vote on the floor of Congress, but once the danger had passed, the coalition was dissolved.

It's not hard to see how influential such coalitions are. To do so, imagine you're a legislative director for a member of Congress. You're charged with preparing a recommended position on what may seem to you like an obscure religious liberty bill. You've had visits with a few constituents who gave you their opinion, you've met with a couple organizations who gave you talking-points memos to help you see their point of view, and you also met with lobbyists who came to you on behalf of a coalition with a hundred organizations who together represent thousands, maybe millions, of your constituents. That last group gave you a letter signed by all of the organizations in the coalition that offers a diverse set of reasoning that points toward a recommended position for your boss to take. That's persuasiveness taken to a whole new level, and it's why such coalitions work.

When I lobbied regularly with the Coalition Against Religious Discrimination (CARD), which is still very active today, our team successfully stopped all of George W. Bush's faith-based initiatives from being legislated into law. Bush still enacted much of his governmental intrusion into religion via executive orders, but those at least could be reversed someday by a future president who is committed to keeping religion and government separate. By stopping legislation, a victory was won that seeded the ground for a better future.

The American Humanist Association participates in several progressive and secular coalitions that work to ensure church-state separation and the implementation of humanist values in public policy. These coalitions include, but are not limited to, CARD, the Coalition for Liberty and Justice, the National Coalition for Public Education, the International Religious Freedom Roundtable, the Leadership Conference on Civil and Human Rights, and the Washington Interreligious Staff Community. The latter has a special quarterly meeting of the Heads of Washington Offices (HOWO) of the various religious groups, only open to top-level staff so that decisions about collaborations can be made on the spot.

I first gained access to the HOWO meetings when I was a board member of Equal Partners in Faith, an edgy early effort to bring together progressives of all religious backgrounds, including those who were nonreligious. When I became executive director for the American Humanist Association, the group would periodically vote to see if it was still appropriate for me to be there, always deciding to keep the door open for my attendance even though the AHA wasn't a religious organization itself. Seeing the effectiveness of these meetings, and the comparative disarray that I saw in the humanist/atheist/freethought movement, I organized the first meeting of the heads of nontheist organizations in 2005, just before George W. Bush's second inauguration, so that we could coordinate to stop Bush's advancement of religion into government. The meeting saw about two dozen organizational leaders in attendance and went on to become an annual event.

Many of these coalitions are made up of groups that disagree on many issues but have agreed to set aside their differences to promote the coalition's shared aim. That's one reason why progressive religious advocacy organizations are frequent coalition partners. Even though they hold differing theological views, they hold some of the same policy goals as many nontheist groups. By working through these coalitions the AHA frequently partners with a variety of faith groups, including Catholics, Baptists, Methodists, Jews, Muslims, Hindus, Buddhists, Baha'is, Sikhs, and even Scientologists.

One of the few problems faced in these coalition meetings and advocacy efforts revolves around language. According to Matthew Bulger, "Many of these groups have worked in coordination for years without a humanist or nontheist contingent, and so while these coalitions are excited to be able to broaden their membership, some explanation is required in making sure coalition language properly reflects all aspects of their membership."

Typically, coalition letters to government officials will begin by mentioning that the coalition comprises faith leaders and other advocacy professionals. Obviously, humanists and other nontheists are reticent to designate their convictions as a variety of "faith," and so broadening this language to include nontheistic leaders is one of the first things that the AHA sets out to do. Assuming the language of coalition letters is within acceptable boundaries, the AHA is excited to work with our religious allies on issues of the day. As an example, Bulger joined a coalition of religious leaders from several Christian and Jewish denominations to lobby the Washington, DC city council to approve the Death with Dignity Act. According to Bulger, "The lobbying event itself was truly a reflection of American religious pluralism. I was able to lobby for this important bill making my humanist identity clear, while standing next to Catholic and Episcopalian priests. Our ability to come together in support of this bill regardless of our different theological views showed the council just how wide public support was for this bill."

The legislation, which passed and is now enacted, builds upon efforts in states like Oregon and Washington, which already had laws on the books to allow compassionate choice at the end of a person's life. These laws propose a commonsense approach to the topic of death with dignity, requiring patients who wish to receive the necessary dtugs to meet several restrictive criteria. It's an issue important to many AHA members, such as Sharon Fratepietro from South Carolina, who seeks to expand such laws to her state. Her letter about this topic published in the *Post and Courier* reads, "It should be a human right for people suffering unbearably from a terminal illness to get medical help to end their lives."

Our continuing work with these coalitions not only helps expedite legislation humanists support or block legislation that humanists don't want, but also helps establish a humanist presence within the greater DC lobbying community, which can lead to increased opportunities for cooperation and mutual success.

Lobbying for Humanist Protections Globally

One relationship that the AHA has taken pains to cultivate is with the foreign affairs committees in both the U.S. House and Senate. The AHA worked for years on international religious freedom issues, which falls within the legislative jurisdiction of the respective foreign affairs committees, and AHA staff has developed lasting personal relationships with those who work on such committees.

Matthew Bulger worked with the House Foreign Affairs Committee, including both Democratic and Republican staffs, to ensure that the Frank R. Wolf International Religious Freedom Act included nontheists and addressed the concerns of the nontheistic community. The Act, also known as HR 1150, does several things, including giving the U.S. administration and the State Department new political tools through increased funding, strengthening the standing of the International Religious Freedom Office and the Ambassador-at-Large for International Religious Freedom, and creating a "Special Watch List" and automatic downgrade to a Country of Particular Concern for nations on the list for three straight years. The legislation also requires the designation of violent nonstate actors who work to weaken religious freedom as "Entities of Particular Concern" and directs the U.S. president to focus sanctions on individuals who carry out or order religious restrictions.

Bulger was able to convince both the Republican and Democratic staffers on the committee to include language that protects not just theistic religious minority communities, but for the first time ever, nontheistic minorities as well. As a result, the Act begins, "The freedom of thought, conscience, and religion is understood to protect theistic and non-theistic beliefs as well as the right not to profess or practice any religion." The Act also condemns "specific targeting of non-theists, humanists, and atheists because of their beliefs" and attempts to forcibly compel "non-believers or non-theists to recant their beliefs or to convert." According to Bulger, "What was required in this case was explaining to staff that the existing laws and policies didn't do enough to specifically include nontheists and their concerns, which is part of the reason why the U.S. government hasn't fully responded to cases of atheist discrimination abroad, including the murder of American atheist Dr. Avijit Roy by religious extremists in Bangladesh." Once that crucial information had been passed along to receptive staff, all that was required was crafting inclusive language which wouldn't upset either party but which would still protect some of the most vulnerable people around the world.

Bulger also worked with those in the office of U.S. Rep. Don Beyer (D-VA) to introduce legislation that prevents immigrants from being denied entry into the United States because of their religious or nonreligious convictions. Bulger met with Beyer's staff to modify the legislation so as to ensure that the rights of nonreligious individuals were included in this bill. As a result of his efforts, the Freedom of Religion Act of 2016 specifically states that "an alien [someone who isn't a U.S. citizen] may not be denied admission to the United States because of the alien's religion or lack of religious beliefs."

Because of his hard work on the bill, Bulger was invited to attend a press conference with Rep. Beyer on Capitol Hill to introduce the legislation. According to Bulger, "This bill represents a significant step for the humanist movement. The specific mention of protection for those without any religion demonstrates that Congress is beginning to expand its understanding of religious freedom to include those who do not identify with any religion."

In both these cases of successful groundbreaking advocacy, what was required for humanists, atheists, and other nontheists to be included in the legislation of the day was a concerted outreach effort by the AHA's lobbyist who had already built key relationships on Capitol Hill. No special favors had to be called in, and humanists didn't have to mount a public campaign to be included in these bills. Arguably, a public campaign would have been detrimental in this case since it would have awoken the Religious Right to our pending success. Instead, Congress was directly shown that humanists are committed to increasing our protection from those around the world who would deny our freedom from religion. We also made it easy for them to do the right thing by showing how to include protections for humanists and other nontheists in the legislation. What resulted was as inclusive and productive as possible.

Lobbying the Executive Branch

The amount of support Donald Trump gave to the Religious Right as president cannot be overestimated. Writing for the *Guardian*, Jessica Glenza explains how this was exemplified by U.S. Secretary of Health and Human Services Alex Azar when he spoke of his government agency as "the department of life, from conception until natural death." Even Religious Right icon Ralph Reed noted, the access "has been remarkable." As Rachel Laser, president and CEO of Americans United for the Separation of Church and State, said after hearing the administration would permit a faith-based foster care agency in South Carolina to deny service to same-sex couples and non-Christians, "The Trump administration uses religion to advance a regressive political agenda that harms others."

While it may seem pointless to lobby a White House with someone like Trump in residence, there are some approaches that are feasible. Upon his election, progressives shifted gears to confront his regressive policies that threatened to drag our country backward. We organized, rallied, resisted, and creatively opposed Trump's agenda. From working to prevent the repeal of the Johnson Amendment (discussed in chapter 10) to challenging the assault on transgender rights, the American Humanist Association and both its nontheistic and theistic allies defended the First Amendment and did our best to protect the rights of those being targeted for discrimination. But even in a hostile political climate, there are still opportunities to advance our agenda. In order to get things done and help those who can be helped, we searched for areas ripe for bipartisan consensus.

One such unifying issue was the struggle for international religious freedom. Democrats and Republicans are often at odds when debating domestic religious liberty issues, such as those related to religious displays on government property, but religious freedom on the international scale often unites Americans. The willingness of religious conservatives in Congress to work with progressive humanists on the Frank Wolf International Religious Freedom Act bill (now law) showed the depth of agreement on this issue. Former Kansas Governor Sam Brownback, Trump's nomination for Ambassador-at-Large for International Religious Freedom, indicated a willingness to meet with humanist and religious progressives, even before being confirmed. Disagreements on many domestic issues don't necessarily prohibit mutual participation on some international concerns, and thus politicians and political appointees who are religious conservatives needn't immediately be written off by liberals for their views.

Humanists and both progressive and conservative theists should work to build on past successes related to international religious freedom. We should work together to remove blasphemy laws in countries that maintain them, seek asylum for those who are threatened, and help change the conditions in countries that lead to the persecution of those of minority faiths and philosophies.

International religious freedom isn't the only issue on which many Republicans and Democrats can work together. Take, for example, the criminal justice reform bill, the REDEEM Act, introduced by conservative U.S. Senator Rand Paul (R-KY) and progressive U.S. Senator Cory Booker (D-NJ). The REDEEM Act would help people convicted of nonviolent crimes to reenter society, would restrict solitary confinement of juveniles, and would combat racial and gender disparities in the criminal justice system. Republicans and Democrats may also find some agreement on fixing voting rights. For example, Rep. Jim Sensenbrenner (R-WI) and Rep. John Conyers (D-MI) reintroduced the Voting Rights Amendment Act in 2017 with a slew of bipartisan cosponsors to help improve our often discriminatory voting system.

We shouldn't automatically reject viable opportunities to work with oppositional White House administrations. By working with a coalition of progressives and conservatives on bipartisan issues, we can create worthwhile change where it's needed. The unrelenting lobbying of the Executive Branch better prepares us to make strides when there's a change in administration and new prospects open up. As advocates, we have a responsibility to oppose regressive policies, but we also have an equal obligation to put our differences aside and work together when possible.

What You Can Do

In addition to the AHA and its Center for Freethought Equality lobbying arm, be sure to support the Secular Coalition for America and lobby groups that work on our specific causes, like Americans United for Separation of Church and State, the Center for Election Science, Population Connection, and Compassion & Choices.

If you want to do the lobbying yourself, visiting a member of Congress or their staff can be an empowering experience and will likely have more impact than anything else you can do as an individual. By engaging in two-way communication, you might sway their thinking. Visits can be done in district when the member is home or on Capitol Hill in their offices. Both the AHA and the SCA hold annual lobby days, as do other issue-based organizations that you may be interested in. These consist of coming to Washington, DC, receiving special training and instructions in a group, and attending multiple planned lobby meetings in congressional offices accompanied by organizational staff. Such days send a strong signal to Capitol Hill staff that this cause is one being promoted by an organized base of constituents whose concerns they'd do well to pay close attention to. Even if you can't make lobby days, be sure to let organizations like the AHA know if you're coming to Washington, DC, since they may be able to arrange for lobby meetings apart from an organized day.

Sometimes even better than a visit to the offices is an organized appearance at a town-hall type event that politicians occasionally hold in their districts—if a dozen show to one of these events with the plan to focus on one issue—or a set of issues—they'll get considerable attention. Or, if you can go to campaign or other events where you may need to financially contribute to attend, you may discover even greater access and interest in your opinions. You might even consider extending friendly invitations to staffers to attend a constituent event or even to come to you to meet with local organizational leaders. It's hard to beat the convincing nature of having someone meet with your leadership core and see your local group in action.

If a face-to-face meeting isn't an option, the next best way to provide influence is through a phone call where you can still spend time explaining your position and get a response from staff. Phone calls are great even on the day of a vote. Positions stated on the calls are tallied so that politicians have a sense of where their constituents stand.

If calls aren't an available option, and you have the time, the next best method is a personal and fully individualized snail-mailed letter. These have a slight edge on emails for influencing members of Congress, because they prompt the offices receiving them to send you a response, sometimes crafted just for you, and that gets them thinking about your point. But keep in mind that snail mail takes a long time, not just because of the postal mail process, but also because letters to members of Congress go through security protocols. That's one reason why emails can be more immediately effective.

Now that congressional offices have developed systems for receiving and tallying emails, their speed and clear usage make them quite useful. You can send them individualized emails via their preferred web-form or email address, or customize e-messages to them via an organization's system—such as when you respond to email action alerts from the AHA. They arrive quickly and get tallied quickly. Social media approaches to members of Congress and their staffs via official Facebook pages provide a growing source of connection. With some principals handling their own Twitter accounts, carefully constructed tweets can also have more impact than traditional means.

While not useless, direct-mail postcards that you send to a sponsoring organization, which then forwards them en masse to an official, are likely the least effective means. The process is slow and bulk deliveries don't normally elicit individual responses. However, sometimes photographs or videos of these bulk mailings can make a nice media statement.

However you choose to engage in the lobbying process, know that your voice is being heard, and matters.

* * *

Recommended Reading

Pasquale Annicchino, *Law and International Religious Freedom* (Routledge, 2019).

Jessica Glenza, "How the Religious Right Gained Unprecedented Access to Trump," *Guardian*, January 31, 2019. www.theguardian.com/us-news/2019/jan/30/donald-trump-administration-religious-right-access

Rebecca H. Gordon and Thomas M. Susman, *The Lobbying Manual: A Complete Guide to Federal Lobbying Law and Practice*, 5th ed. (ABA Book Publishing, 2016).

Rep. Mike Honda, "Recognizing the National Day of Reason," *Congressional Record*, April 25, 2013. www.govinfo.gov/content/pkg/CREC-2013-04-25/pdf/CREC-2013-04-25-pt1-PgE545-4.pdf

Amanda Knief, *The Citizen Lobbyist: A How-to Manual for Making Your Voice Heard in Government* (Pitchstone Publishing, 2013).

David Nelson and Susan Webb Yackee, "Lobbying Coalitions and Government Policy Change: An Analysis of Federal Agency Rulemaking," *Journal of Politics* 74, no. 2 (2012).

Pew Research Center, "Nones on the Rise," October 9, 2012. www.pewforum.org/Unaffiliated/nones-on-the-rise.aspx

Tricia Tongco and Emily Ellsworth, "How to Make Your Congressman Listen to You," *ATTN: Inc.*, November 13, 2016. www.attn.com/stories/12768/former-congressional-staffer-explains-how-to-make-congressman-listen

3

HUMANIST POLITICIANS

* * *

When looking at the political picture today, it often seems like we have to choose the lesser of two (or more) evils. There aren't enough consistently high-integrity politicos, and too many of them don't share our humanist values. In 2016, a number of humanists were so disappointed with the failure of the humanistic U.S. Senator Bernie Sanders to win the Democratic nomination that they considered voting for third-party candidates who better represented their values rather than Sanders' recommendation, U.S. Secretary of State Hillary Clinton. I voted for Clinton, but I am familiar with the drive to vote for the candidate who represents the closest match to your views. For example, I voted for Green Party candidate Ralph Nader over then Vice President Al Gore in the 2000 presidential election.

Back in 2000 I wasn't thrilled with President Bill Clinton's record, which too often seemed to cater to the rich, such as his willingness to deregulate Wall Street and repeal the Glass-Steagall Act. While his administrations could have been worse, he consistently failed to meet my high expectations for his presidency. His administrations failed to enact pro-LGBTQ laws, increased the scope of George H. W. Bush's war on drugs and crime, and introduced the first faith-based initiative in a program called Charitable Choice. Though Gore got much better postelection as an advocate for addressing climate change, he wasn't the picture of liberal inspiration during the 2000 campaign.

I was intrigued by Nader's openly humanist approach. After I attended a Rally for Nader at the DC Convention Center, where he was joined by Phil Donahue, Michael Moore, and Rage Against the Machine, I was convinced Nader could make a difference for the better. Of course, that election held many lessons for us, from reminding us that the Electoral College, not the popular vote, chooses the president, to the realization that third-party votes can swing a close election in the favor of one's least favorite candidate. Eight long years with George W. Bush as "religious-leader-in-chief" clarified the situation better than ever.

When considering the 2016 presidential election, many humanists were similarly disappointed with the options. Not only was Bernie Sanders' loss to Hillary Clinton in the primary a significant factor for some, but so was Sanders' treatment by the Democratic Party, as it was revealed in a story by John Uchill and Harper Neidig in *The Hill* that some in the party were bent on using his lack of fervent religiosity as a chance to attack him as an atheist. The Democratic National Committee did act appropriately to address the poor behavior of its staff, but it was a timely reminder of how deeply ingrained the prejudice against nontheists is.

Some, like philosophers Noam Chomsky and John Halle, have discussed the value of lesser-evil voting, convincingly directing us to the best moral choice. The essence of the argument is that no matter how favorably inclined we are to protesting various wrongs, a protest vote doesn't make sense. Voting via secret ballot, your actual vote cast for an unwinnable candidate doesn't bolster your values. Rather, doing so just makes the election of the person you least support a little more likely to win. Assuming that candidate is a Republican, as was the case with me in 2000, they'll likely go on to push backward policies on climate, immigrant rights, reproductive choice, separation of church and state, and many other issues of concern to humanists.

Win-Win Choices

Fortunately, there's a growing number of good choices we can make in the voting booth. Just a few years ago, there were only a handful of elected officials at local, state, and national levels who identified with the nontheist community via some name, be it humanist, atheist, agnostic, or freethinker. But that number is rapidly increasing. As I write there are sixty such politicians holding office in state and federal levels, and many more planning to run for office. Some folks are rising through the ranks from entry-level offices to state houses to state senates, with aspirations for Capitol Hill. Most of them are supported by the Freethought Equality Fund PAC, which seeks to increase the number of open humanists and atheists in public office. Among them are some terrific individuals from many diverse backgrounds.

Perhaps the most long-standing example is Ernie Chambers. An AHA Lifetime Achievement Awardee, Chambers emerged as a leader for the community in Omaha, Nebraska, speaking up for the rights of those who were downtrodden. A state senator for Nebraska's 11th District for decades, Chambers spearheaded moves to abolish corporal punishment in schools, afford equal state pensions to women, and switch to district-based voting to give Black and Brown citizens a fair shot at election to public office. He also deserves credit for convincing Nebraska to be one of the first conservative-minded states to abolish the death penalty. As he concisely stated on winning one of a number of awards, "As an elected official, I know the difference between theology and politics. My interest is in legislation, not salvation."

Juan Mendez served as an open atheist for two terms in the Arizona State House of Representatives (2013–2016), where he was a leader of the Arizona Legislative Latino Caucus, before being elected as a state senator for Arizona's 26th District. Mendez has sponsored legislation to support end-of-life choices, equal rights for women, and the separation of church and state. Before running for office, Mendez ran the local nonprofit program Arizona Community Voicemail, connecting the homeless and economically vulnerable to jobs, housing, and hope. Today when he isn't at the legislature or in the community he is a substitute high school teacher for the Tempe and Mesa school districts.

Audra Killingsworth is a newly elected town council member in Apex, North Carolina. Early in her political career, Killingsworth grew up poor in a small, rural town in Louisiana and put herself through college where she studied occupational therapy. In addition to her elected position she's a rehab director at an independent living facility and volunteers at a local food bank. Identifying publicly as a humanist, Killingsworth didn't run on faith but instead appealed to the public's desire for someone who listens, wants solutions, and has a vision for the future. Instead of suggesting she was a god's chosen candidate, she made a commitment to always be honest, to be available to constituents, and to work toward keeping the town a wonderfully diverse, inclusive place to live and raise a family.

We've had very few federal level politicians in our nation's history that self-categorized themselves with one or more of the various nontheistic labels. Thomas Paine was a founding father, but never an office holder. While he was an intellectual forerunner to modern humanists and was explicitly anti-Christian, he was reluctant to identify as an atheist. Whenever the charge of atheism was made on him, he countered that he believed in a creator god, preferring an explicit deism to the negative perception of atheism.

Some thought Thomas Jefferson to be a humanist, and while he had some humanist leanings including skepticism of supernatural phenomena, he was at most a kindred spirit of sorts. Jefferson argued against the publication of Paine's *The Age of Reason*, supported the continuation of the institution of slavery, and identified as a believer. That doesn't mean we can't celebrate his achievements in church-state separation, but we need not convert those who came before us into the perfect humanists they weren't. Rather, we can accept that our ideas drew from great thinkers of the past who themselves were flawed.

Labeling oneself a humanist is no safeguard at all against racism or other forms of bigotry. But being a good/perfect/ideal humanist as we define it helps prevent movement toward bigotry because it means that you not only embrace the foundational principles of compassion, empathy, egalitarianism, and reason, but also that you do the hard work to constantly self-educate about inequities and why they exist. Self-improvement, especially as it relates to self-education, is a longstanding humanist tradition, even if it is not always codified into identity statements. What's needed now is for those who call themselves "humanist" to more universally get with the program, educate, and wake up to the antiracist and other egalitarian policies that flow from humanism.

Robert Green Ingersoll, known as the "Great Agnostic," was a popular orator in the late 1800s. While he was fully open about his progressive humanism and agnosticism, being one of the first public figures to fully embrace humanistic ideas, he never ran for public office. President William Howard Taft was a Unitarian and endured numerous controversies about his religion and possible lack of faith. While it's hard to say what he really believed, he was clearly not an open nontheist. Writing in a letter explaining why he wouldn't accept an offer of presidency at Yale University, he said, "I believe in God. I do not believe in the Divinity of Christ, and there are many other of the postulates of the orthodox creed to which I cannot subscribe. I am not, however, a scoffer at religion but on the contrary recognize, in the fullest manner, the elevating influence that it has had and always will have in the history of mankind."

With women not even allowed to vote in America until the 1920s, there wasn't opportunity for nontheist women to hold public office in the nation's first 150 years. But if that had been a possibility, a number of prominent female thought leaders would have made great politicians, such as Elizabeth Cady Stanton and Susan B. Anthony. Later humanist women leaders like Margaret Sanger and Helen Keller were significant political figures in their time, even if they never held political office, as was Shirley Chisholm, who became the first Black woman elected to Congress.

Among the first openly nontheist people to serve in a higher office in the United States was Jesse Ventura, who served as governor of Minnesota from 1999 to 2003. Ventura was an outsider to politics in many ways, being a libertarian, a former World Wrestling Federation wrestler, and someone never afraid to speak his mind. Considering his many divergent views, his atheism didn't receive as much publicity as one might expect.

Pete Stark of California was the first member of Congress in history to come out as a nontheist, which he did during his eighteenth term of office in his liberal district south of San Francisco. Others had come out after leaving public office, such as former U.S. Representative

Barney Frank of Massachusetts, but doing so clearly, and while in office, and then successfully running for reelection as Stark did, was groundbreaking. At the behest of a contest devised by David Niose, then a board member of the AHA, the Secular Coalition for America sought the highest-ranking politician in the United States willing to publicly identify as a nontheist. Stark reported back to SCA staff that he identified as a Unitarian and was willing to be open about his lack of a belief in any higher power. When he finally did so in March 2007, it immediately made headline news, news that carried on for days after the AHA ran a large display ad in the *Washington Post* congratulating Stark for coming out.

Stark was praised by progressives for his honesty and berated by conservatives for his lack of religiosity. But he handily won reelection, with seemingly no ill effects from his announcement of nontheism. He lost a later election to a popular young fellow Democrat, but the deciding factor appeared unrelated to religion or belief. While Stark proved that not believing in God wasn't an absolute barrier to public office, the sense that atheism was political suicide did not yet fade from Capitol Hill. In fact, it was over a decade later when Rep. Huffman became the second member of Congress to come out forthrightly as a humanist and a nonbeliever while still in office. Representing California's 2nd District, which follows the coast north of San Francisco, Rep. Huffman is a true champion for humanist principles.

In this modern age we also have examples of politicians who appear to follow humanist values, but who haven't made a public statement about their position on the existence of gods and other supernatural forces. U.S. Senator Kyrsten Sinema (D-AZ) was a celebrated member of the humanist community before running for Congress. She spoke at multiple movement conferences, including the AHA's annual conference, and local group events. But during the campaign, when humanists and atheists started spreading the news that a nontheist was about to be elected, Sinema's spokesperson clarified her position, stating, "Kyrsten believes the terms non-theist, atheist or nonbeliever are not befitting of her life's work or personal character. She does not identify as any of the above."

Her record as a congressperson has been mixed from a humanist perspective. She voted for a resolution that supported adding a prayer to the U.S. Capitol Museum. She voted to pass the Thin Blue Line Act, to help prosecutors seek the death penalty for people who attempt to kill first responders. And she voted for numerous pieces of anti-immigrant legislation, from "Kate's Law" to the Make America Secure Act, which gives funding for the border wall, to the Verify First Act, which requires citizenship verification before people can access the Affordable Care Act. Though Sinema often votes in humanistic directions, and did choose to swear in on the Constitution instead of a bible, she's not (yet?) an open nontheist in public office.

There are also a number of technically religiously unaffiliated members of Congress. Most of them, however, are widely known to be Christian, and the few who may be nontheists have said nothing publicly to confirm that possibility.

That takes us to the career of Jamie Raskin.

Jamie Raskin

Jamie Raskin provides a model for what a modern politician could aspire to be, not just for humanist politicians, but for any politician. Raskin maintains a steadfast commitment to his principles, balancing them appropriately with his need to represent all his constituents and the interests of broader society. When accepting the Humanist Distinguished Service Award from the AHA in 2008, Raskin demonstrated his commitment to reason and progressive values, saying,

> Defending humanist values and secular democracy in public settings has very little to do with courage and everything to do with *self-respect* and the gut instinct that we allow unreason to control public decision-making only at our own risk and peril. As Voltaire shrewdly put it, "Anyone who can make you believe absurdities can make you commit atrocities."

A firm supporter of First Amendment freedoms of and from religion, he added that "the promotion of religious dogma and sectarianism through government continues to be a paradigm force undermining public reason," and that we have "a responsibility to place the actual well-being of humanity at the forefront of the public agenda. This is the true moral imperative of our time."

Raskin, born December 13, 1962, in Washington, DC, comes from an impressive line of politically active people. His grandfather, attorney Samuel Bellman, was Minnesota's first Jewish state legislator, elected in 1935. His mother, Barbara Bellman Raskin, was a novelist and journalist, and his father, Marcus Raskin, was aide to President John F. Kennedy and a member of his National Security Council. His father also cofounded the Institute for Policy Studies, a progressive think tank. After graduating from Georgetown Day School, Jamie Raskin pursued a degree at Harvard University, graduating *magna cum laude* in 1983, and graduating *magna cum laude* again, this time, from Harvard Law School, in 1987. After holding positions such as assistant attorney general in Massachusetts and general counsel for Jesse Jackson's Rainbow Coalition, Raskin consulted for Yale Law School while teaching constitutional law for twenty-five years at American University's Washington College of Law. Raskin decided to run for the 20th District of the Maryland State Senate in 2006, successfully defeating a thirty-two-year incumbent who was also President Pro Tempore of the Maryland Senate. Raskin's victory was a landslide, as he defeated his opponent with 67 percent of the vote.

Already influential in the field of constitutional law, authoring multiple volumes on the subject and helping found the acclaimed Marshall-Brennan Constitutional Literacy Project, Raskin refused to rest on his laurels, partaking in remarkable fights for the rights of Marylanders. In this age of politics, where religion plays a more pivotal role than ever before, it is rare to see a candidate boldly represent the views of true progressives like humanists, but that's what Raskin did in the Maryland Senate. In his time as a state senator, Raskin ascended to Majority Whip and passed over a hundred bills, delivering on his promise to reform the state of Maryland.

Raskin passionately advocated for marriage equality and testified in the Maryland Senate on the subject, even before being elected to office. In a legislative hearing on a proposed constitutional amendment to prohibit gay marriage, Raskin responded to Maryland State Senator Nancy Jacobs (R), who said the Bible reserved marriage for a man and a woman. Raskin said, "Senator, when you took your oath of office, you placed your hand on the Bible and swore to uphold the Constitution. You didn't put your hand on the Constitution and swear to uphold the Bible." Once elected Raskin introduced and helped pass the first measure of any state in the United States to realize marriage equality reform without any prior judicial ruling striking it down.

Furthering his goal to create gender parity, Raskin passed legislation that provided reasonable accommodation for pregnant women at work, strengthened equal pay for equal work, and exposed pregnancy crisis centers that seek to religiously misinform and shame women into limiting their reproductive choices. Raskin additionally degendered girls and boys programs in juvenile detention, disrupting the existing system that tracked boys toward auto repair and physical education and girls toward cosmetology or home economics. Continuing to build on his commitments, Raskin introduced legislation that protected the rights of victims of race and gender discrimination by expanding employment discrimination law remedies and ensuring a trial by jury in the state court system where they were not previously permitted. He achieved passage of the Freedom of Political Expression and Assembly Act, which prevented police from spying on political organizations without suspicion of any wrongdoing.

Raskin's humanistic views extend to environmentalism as well. He made considerable efforts to address climate change, helping to dramatically decrease emissions in the state of Maryland. Also aiding local farmers, Raskin introduced a farm-to-schools program that provides public schools with local food and produce, keeping the local economy strong while also piquing community interest in local businesses and fostering a better communal environment. In addition, all state facilities are now mandated to compost, recycle, and comply with state green purchasing rules, while implementing strict legal liability on all fracking in the state.

An ardent proponent of criminal justice reform, Raskin worked to successfully abolish the Maryland death penalty in 2013. Despite being a self-described "strong Democrat," Raskin also has a long history of working across party lines, passing a bipartisan bill that reviewed mandatory minimums in drug cases, along with the Maryland Second Chance Act, so that those with nonviolent misdemeanors do not have to disclose their conviction to the public if they have been clean for three years. In an effort to deemphasize nonviolent crimes, Raskin passed a bill that legalized medicinal marijuana, and was supportive of Maryland's efforts to decriminalize cannabis. Raskin took on the big liquor lobbyists, working with Mothers Against Drunk Driving (who named Raskin a legislator of the year in 2016) to require convicted drunk drivers to use ignition interlock breathalyzers, which has significantly lowered alcohol-related traffic fatalities in Maryland.

Raskin has helped secure voting rights for ex-felons, lowered the voting registration age to sixteen so high schoolers can register, and organized a signed letter to Congress asking to repeal *Citizens United*. He sponsored legislation that helped Maryland be the first of what is now a dozen states that guarantee its electoral votes to the presidential candidate who receives the most popular votes in all fifty states and Washington, DC.

And while the list of impressive gains is too long to include here in its entirety, I'd be remiss not to mention how Raskin helped Maryland become the first state to recognize benefit corporations, which are a relatively new form of corporation that allows them to pursue socially responsible purposes in addition to profits—an important breakthrough since standard corporations can actually be successfully sued by their stock holders if the corporation pursues public good over profit. Raskin also championed transparency, holding state representatives more accountable on spending, so that all expenditures over $10,000 must be online for all to see.

Due to his exemplary work in the Maryland State Senate, Raskin became known as one of the nation's most talented and responsive legislators. And he has long embodied his humanism in his personal life as well. He's a supportive, egalitarian-minded husband to his wife, Sarah Bloom Raskin, who is a figure of importance as well, having served as the Maryland Commissioner of Financial Regulation, as a governor of the Federal Reserve Board, and as the U.S. Deputy Secretary of the Treasury during the Obama administration. This progressive power couple has three children already with promising paths of their own. One of them has even given an impressive spoken word presentation at an AHA conference.

Having accomplished much in Maryland, Raskin saw the need to spread the positive impact across the country. So when the opportunity arose, he didn't hesitate to add his name to the ballot for the 8th Congressional District. Raskin succeeded against the odds in the most expensive primary campaign in U.S. congressional history. Outspent by record levels and facing candidates with deeper pockets and longer careers, Raskin consistently connected with people, many of whom were already impressed with his work in the Maryland State Senate as a champion of rights for all. His stellar record, along with his strong grassroots support, helped him win the primary.

Then, on November 8, 2016, Raskin was elected to the House of Representatives with 60 percent of the vote and laid out extensive plans for the forthcoming years. Raskin said he wanted to continue his fight for green energy and put a price on the "social calamity" of carbon. In addition, he wanted to reduce gun violence and challenge the National Rifle Association's deplorable tactics. Raskin hoped to lift wages and benefits across the board for *all* Americans to increase economic opportunity. Hoping to work with both Democrats and Republicans, Raskin wanted to protect women's health choices, describing himself as "100 percent pro-choice." Raskin also hoped to continue his efforts to repeal *Citizens United*.

Citing public health as a priority, Raskin said he hoped to expand and protect Medicare and Social Security for those who have earned it. He also wanted to promote education and work for the success of all students. He affirmed his aim to defend the Constitution against the Religious Right, who wish to repeal measures that provide equality for all Americans, such as the 2015 ruling on same-sex marriage. Raskin wished to build on his success with Maryland's DREAM Act, allowing a path to legal citizenship. He also hoped to build on his legacy of decency toward those who've given our country their military service, where in Maryland he provided housing, educational, and employment opportunities for Maryland's veterans.

As a strong proponent of LGBTQ rights, Raskin also wanted to ensure anti-LGBTQ discrimination is written out of the law across the United States. On an international level, Raskin said he would pursue nuclear non-proliferation, preventing Iran and other dangerous countries from obtaining nuclear weapons. Raskin hoped to build on the success of his equal pay for equal work legislation in Maryland by championing the rights of individuals and their right to unionize. A vegetarian for the past decade, Raskin also believes in protecting the rights and welfare of nonhuman animals.

As a new member of Congress, Raskin wasted no time in hitting the ground running. He quickly joined colleagues in raising questions about the 2016 presidential election, raising concerns about voter suppression and the apparent Russian interference in the campaign. The Senate failed to join the House in these concerns, but they laid the groundwork for further action in the coming months. Raskin then cosponsored the Presidential Disclosure of Foreign Business Transactions Act, and he cosponsored a bill (HR-1987, which now has 59 other cosponsors) that would create a congressional oversight commission that could declare the president physically or mentally incapacitated, leading to their removal from office under the 25th Amendment of the U.S. Constitution.

In his first term of office, he involved himself in a number of key congressional committees. Raskin is the Vice-Ranking Member of the House Judiciary Committee and serves as the Ranking Member of the Subcommittee on Intergovernmental Affairs within the House Oversight and Government Reform Committee. He's also the Congressional Progressive Caucus Vice Chair and Liaison to New Members, and a Senior Whip for the House Democratic Caucus.

Beginning his congressional championship of religion-government separation, Raskin cosponsored House Resolution 349, which calls for the global repeal of blasphemy, heresy, and apostasy laws. He sponsored amendments that would enforce the Clean Air Act and address ethics issues. The breadth and progressive activist nature of Raskin's choices for action demonstrate how he considers the realistic options before us, refuses to be constrained by tradition, and weighs the consequences not just for himself, but for others as well. Affectionately called "the professor" by his colleagues, he's respected for the deep research and understanding he brings to the table.

To ensure that his message and goals are handed down to the next generation, Raskin sponsors Democracy Summer programs that provide intensive civics education to high school and college students and trains them in door-to-door education and advocacy to help other progressive candidates win their campaigns and add more progressive voices to Congress.

Through his work Raskin proves himself to be a staunch protector of rights, proponent of justice, supporter of public health, defender of the Constitution, and so much more. Raskin once told me that he's a Jew in his heart and a humanist in his head because, while he continues to embrace Judaism for himself and his family, his theological and societal approach is one that is in line with humanism. Raskin may be a skeptic when it comes to extraordinary and unproven claims, but he is a believer in freedom, social responsibility, and the pursuit of knowledge.

America needs more politicians like Raskin who place the collective gain of all Americans over personal gain. And we can work toward that goal in a number of ways, from supporting the candidacies of visionary politicians, becoming candidates ourselves, and perhaps, most importantly, realizing that we are each responsible for performing our civic duties. Whether we're lobbying, speaking out publicly, or simply being informed voters on election day, we have to participate. We can't expect our leaders to accomplish lasting substantive change without our involvement and support.

A Future of Humanist Politicians

One can envision a future where a majority of our politicians are humanists. It would undoubtedly be a significant divergence from today's world where politicians are frequently seen as weak-willed, money-chasing, arrogant elites who will say anything to garner favor, including scapegoating women and minorities. A humanist identity doesn't automatically reverse such negative traits, but envisioning genuinely humanist politicians assumes that they fully embrace humanist moral principles and act and behave accordingly.

That means that such a future would be characterized by politicians who are steadfast in their commitments to humanist ideals and accept the responsibility to represent all their constituents. Such high-integrity leaders would help move the nation toward progress on climate issues, immigrant rights, racial equality, reproductive choice, separation of church and state, end-of-life choices, equal rights for women, and many other important concerns of the day. Such politicians would know the difference between theology and politics and never allow their personal faith or the majority faith of their constituents to become government policy. They'd be open and honest about their various nontheistic identities, but these identities wouldn't define them or be something they seek to impose on others. In short, such humanist politicians would be champions for democratic humanistic principles that can be appreciated by all.

* * *

Recommended Reading

Noam Chomsky and John Halle, "An Eight Point Brief for Lesser Evil Voting," JohnHalle.com, June 15, 2016. johnhalle.com/outragesandinterludes/?p=1065

Alex Clearfield, "Raskin Hopes Grass Roots Will Grow to Maryland House Win," *Roll Call*, October 26, 2015. www.rollcall.com/news/home/jamie-raskin-maryland-house-district-8

Caleb Gee, "No, Bill Clinton Was Not a Progressive President," *U.S. Hypocrisy*, August 27, 2015. ushypocrisy.com/2015/08/27/the-true-legacy-of-bill-clintons-presidency-is-not-what-some-progressives-would-have-you-believe/

Senators Lee, Raskin, et al., "Labor and Employment—Equal Pay for Equal Work," *MD Senate Bill 424*, March 5, 2015. mgaleg.maryland.gov/webmga/frmMain.aspx?pid=billpage&tab=subject3&id=sb0424&stab=01&ys=2015RS

John Lewis, *Across That Bridge: Life Lessons and a Vision for Change* (Hachette Books, 2012).

Senators Madaleno, Raskin, et al., "Religious Freedom and Civil Marriage Protection Act," *MD Senate Bill 290*, 2008. mgaleg. maryland.gov/webmga/frmMain.aspx?tab=subject3&ys=2008rs percent2fbillfile percent2fsb0290.htm

Alexandria Ocasio-Cortez, *This Is What I Am* (CreateSpace, 2019).

Wright, Constable, & Skerrn, "Maryland's Employment Discrimination Law Remedies to Be Expanded," October 1, 2007. www. wcslaw.com/marylands-employment-discrimination-law-remedies-to-be-expanded-employers-get-ready/

4

HUMANIST PUBLIC POLICY

* * *

How do we best determine what we aim to achieve with public policy? How do we define who we seek to benefit? How does such a process define the way humanists best consider some of the more "charged" issues of public life? Examining how we can apply humanist principles helps us generalize what humanists *should* (and *should not*) do in relationship to public policy.

Who Are Our Constituents?

When we think about how best to accomplish the common good through public policy advocacy, an important consideration is how we define who the public is that we seek to benefit.

Many religious adherents, to varying degrees, see their faith as the one true path to a god (or gods) and dehumanize those who don't follow their religion. This may be especially true for those in certain religions who read their scripture literally. Consider, as just one example from a major religion, the following from the Christian bible: "If your very own brother, or your son or daughter, or the wife you love, or your closest friend secretly entices you, saying, 'Let us go and worship other gods' . . . do not yield to them or listen to them. Show them no pity. Do not spare them or shield them. You must certainly put them to death." (Deuteronomy 13:6–9) As anyone familiar with world religions knows, this type of scripture is not unique to Christianity.

Indeed, it's not hard to see how traditional religions often demonize outsiders. Whether core to a particular faith or just a means of boosting the growth or longevity of a religion, the exclusivity of such beliefs make some religious adherents poor public policymakers. After all, it's limiting to have the predisposition that the only constituents who matter are those who share your faith. Further limiting their potential as public policymakers is the fact that many religious people see the laws of their faith as more important than the laws of the nation. To cite another passage from the Christian bible, "Peter and the other apostles replied: 'We must obey God rather than human beings!'"(Acts 5:29) Some religious adherents undoubtedly interpret this literally—specifically, that if there's a conflict between human laws and their god's laws, their god's laws are to be obeyed. This presents an obvious conflict for any public official who might subscribe to this view. U.S. oaths of office for state and federal legislators, as well as judges, affirm one's highest allegiance is to the U.S. Constitution, and in many cases, the oaths require allegiance to the laws of the land as well. Are biblical literalists who take such oaths lying, or are they violating their faith's principles?

This challenge of allegiance doesn't necessarily disqualify religious folks from elected positions; after all, the Constitution wisely forbids a religious test for public office. Just as it is unconstitutional to require someone to profess a particular religious belief before they can fill a government post, it is unconstitutional to disqualify someone for not adhering to a particular religious viewpoint. In practice, many individuals who identify with various faith labels don't accept all of their religion's doctrines. Religious politicians can make good public policymakers as long as they are willing to put their constituents, the nation, and the Constitution first. Take, for example, then U.S. presidential candidate John F. Kennedy, who said, "Contrary to common newspaper usage, I am not the Catholic candidate for president. I am the Democratic Party's candidate for president, who happens also to be a Catholic. I do not speak for my church on public matters, and the church does not speak for me." He added that presidents "must neither be humbled by making it the instrument of any one religious group, nor tarnished by arbitrarily withholding its occupancy from the members of any one religious group."

As opposed to those who get their direction from outdated texts and questionable divine revelation, freethinkers have good reasons to believe that commitments to reason, empathy, compassion, and egalitarianism provide the best tools to discerning a better future for everyone. Humanists are understandably just as convinced of the accuracy of their convictions as are people of traditional religious faith. But if they follow their humanist principles assiduously, they won't dehumanize those who disagree with them, and they will accept that others can find ways to do good, even within truth-obscuring faiths. Humanists are also practical; recognizing the minority status of our nontheistic philosophy, we cultivate respect and reciprocity with religious allies who will help us achieve our aspirations for a better world.

Humanists, while grasping the benefits of cultural diversity and endeavoring to be aware of the injustices inflicted on certain groups, aim to see the human race as one people. That's why humanist policy is less about preserving religious or nationalist fervor and more about striving toward universal standards of human and civil rights. That means that we deemphasize pride in community, state, nation, and other such ways of distinguishing "us" from "them." But just because we deemphasize such differences, it doesn't mean we are extinguishing differences or wiping the societal slate clean of injustices.

This is why humanists, while being universalists of sorts, still support Black Lives Matter over All Lives Matter. We've either experienced the discrimination firsthand or done our homework to understand that Black and Brown lives are shamefully devalued in our society. It's all too common to see such folks on the receiving end of physical violence perpetrated by police and other government actors. Those who call for All Lives Matter in such an environment, whether they intend to dismiss real rights struggles or not, send the signal that they are blind to the unequal position different groups in our society face. Being race-neutral in a racist world isn't enough. Leveling the playing field, just like leveling the foundation of a new building, is a prerequisite for building a truly egalitarian society.

A barrier toward working for universal humanity is that humans, by their nature, are categorizing creatures. A study published in the *Journal of Experimental Psychology* confirmed that as we take in the world around us, we naturally seek to match items and place them in categories based on their apparent features. While we might challenge such a process, it's part of how our brains work and so it may take effort to overcome this tendency. Furthermore, we may have many good reasons to take pride in a group to which we belong—for example, in a compassionate family, a progressive community, a resilient cultural group, an environmentally forward-looking state, or an accomplished nation. It makes sense to be appreciative of the positive aspects of a group, which may provide a positive example that others might emulate, but such pride should be measured.

Any sense of self-congratulation should go hand-in-hand with self-criticism and self-education. Undoubtedly, as compassionate as your family might be, it likely has its flaws. As progressive as your community might be, it hasn't achieved its full potential. As resilient as your cultural group might be, it likely has aspects in need of improvement. As environmentally forward-thinking as your state might be, it hasn't solved climate change's challenges. And no matter how accomplished your nation might be, undoubtedly, those accomplishments may have been on the backs of those who didn't fare as well.

Inherent to humanism is our drive toward steady improvement, and when it comes to ourselves, lifelong education must be a priority, not just in the sciences and history, but also in our cultural understandings. Knowing that society is riddled with racism, sexism, and other prejudices, for example, signals us to spend extra effort to strive toward overcoming normative stereotypes.

Of course, we shouldn't forget that different perspectives and approaches are needed if we wish to maximize our potential. Too much unanimity and cultural sameness can open the door to groupthink, demagoguery, and even fascism. Incorporating diverse perspectives into everything we do opens different doors to creativity, improves understanding, and inspires activism.

Where do these considerations lead us? We must first look to ourselves. Starting with never-ending self-education, we also can invite diverse stakeholders who might help lead us toward solutions that will work for them. We can also examine situations to recognize when we should take the lead and when we should follow others and provide support to the best of our abilities. As we get our own house in order, we are far better positioned to make a positive difference in public policy.

This doesn't mean there's only one right answer or that a dogmatic orthodox humanism is a good result. Differing strategies and emphases will exist. Historically, humanists' liberal tendencies pushed us a little too readily toward accepting everyone no matter how they define good. But that's a strategy for blandness, not boldness.

We want to promote public policy that leads to good consequences for as many as possible, not just from our own group, and not even just for our own nation. There's more to the *how* of public policy than the *who*, but already our focus on improving the lot of everyone speaks to a different approach from those who take a narrower view.

How Do We Best Make Public Policy Choices?

In addition to an expansive and just approach to who we benefit, our public policy efforts must not utilize damaging means that work against a progressive vision for the world that we'd like to live in, because the ends, no matter how noble, don't always justify the means. In fact, our understanding of the relationship between ends and means has evolved considerably since Machiavelli's *The Prince*.

As we consider what our goals should be and what we might do to accomplish them, we'd ideally endeavor to study and understand all the potential impacts of both the goals and the methods we might employ on all the potential parties. After all, every move we make has its effects, from the ripples in the water caused by dropping a couple pebbles in a pond to the global generational impacts that followed the decision to drop nuclear bombs on Hiroshima and Nagasaki. That's why even when we get our policy aims right, but don't consider how we get there, we may overlook possible negative consequences. U.S. history is riddled with situations like this: from the compromises to unite all the states of the union that resulted in expanding slavery, to the acquisition of U.S. territories by breaking promises and stealing land from Native Americans, to supporting U.S. oil resource interests in ways that sowed the seeds of hate in many places of the world. On a smaller scale, consider the use of the filibuster in the Senate.

The filibuster (which comes from a Dutch word for "pirate") is a tool that for some serves as a barrier to needed change and for others as a backstop against hasty and detrimental decision-making. In practice, it's carried out by a senator or group of senators who steal the Senate floor and who speak indefinitely on a topic in order to prevent a vote and force their opponents to compromise. In 1917 a rule was added to allow for a two-thirds majority vote for "cloture," which, if successful, would stop the filibuster. But two-thirds votes are hard to achieve.

While used occasionally for liberal ends, the filibuster was used extensively in U.S. history as a drag on progress for the rights of African Americans. It was used to extend slavery, prevent the reversal of Jim Crow laws, and, in an almost successful sixty-day filibuster, nearly stopped the passage of the Civil Rights Act of 1964—during which Senator Strom Thurmond (R-SC) achieved the record for filibustering by speaking for over twenty-four hours. In 1975 the Senate made filibusters a touch easier to stop by reducing the number needed for cloture to three-fifths, or sixty Senators, but they have been used more and more in the twenty-first century, spiking to new heights under President Barack Obama's administration. For instance, the Paycheck Fairness Act, meant to fight gender discrimination in the workplace, was filibustered twice by Republicans in the Senate in 2014, preventing its passage. It's so much part of the legislative process today that a bill rarely goes to a vote unless leadership feels they have a sixty-person majority.

Does the filibuster protect against the tyranny of the majority, or is it an abuse of democracy? Journalist Matthew Yglesias argues effectively in *The Atlantic* that the filibuster is a "procedural rule that facilitates obstruction." While there's some risk in removing the filibuster, particularly a short-term risk for the minority party, that's a risk that is worth the opportunity to see swifter change going forward. During this era of rapid cultural development, technological changes occurring at a blistering pace, and global challenges like climate change, dwindling resources, and terrorism, we need to be accelerating policy change, not holding it back. The filibuster tool is ultimately one that encourages maintaining the status quo, and so it's a tool we're better off without.

But until such time as it can be eliminated, should the filibuster be used? Being a temporary obstructionist in pursuit of respectable aims is not necessarily a morally repugnant choice. It's not analogous to lying or cheating, which degrade our character the more they are employed. And it's not analogous to other harm-causing behavior, since it's not filibustering itself that is the problem—it's the long-term impact of the tool on the legislative progress that's at issue. The remaining danger in using the filibuster is that we will become reliant upon it and work less vigorously to end it. Situations like this are common when we acknowledge that we no longer want a certain tool in our toolbox, but we continue to use the tool until it is actually removed.

A similar example is found in an AHA adjunct organization, the Humanist Society, and its decision to remain a religious organization in order to endorse humanist celebrants to perform legal weddings across the nation. Most self-identifying humanists don't see humanism as a religion, and an argument can be made that some humanists intentionally defining themselves as religious may obscure humanists' collective struggle for equal rights and respect in our society. Preferably there would not be organizations that take advantage of religious status to improve their position and services. But if the Humanist Society didn't exist, humanists and atheists in a number of states might feel forced to participate in faith-based ceremonies that are inconsistent with their convictions—it's a lose-lose conundrum.

The ideal solution is to convince government to accept nonreligious organizations as certifying bodies for wedding celebrants, and both the AHA and the Humanist Society support such an end game. That's consistent with the AHA's overall perspective that special rights for religion are unwarranted—they either carve out unfair advantages for the religious or they make exceptions to rules that shouldn't exist in the first place. In this case, the rule that only religious organizations can endorse wedding celebrants gives an unfair advantage to the religious. Until such time as the system can be improved, the Humanist

Society will continue to offer its services, while not passing up any opportunities to seek systemic progress.

As we consider policy choices that will make lives better, we should strive to overcome our various "privileges"—a sociological term highlighting special advantages dominant groups in society have over groups that tend to be recipients of discrimination. We should use scientifically sound research while avoiding pitfalls like conformity, rationalization, oversimplification, unwarranted assumptions, and hasty conclusions. We also must understand how decisions will affect both majorities and minorities. Understanding the potentials that a policy might have, considering the consequences of means employed, and aiming to choose what will be most beneficial for all is the work of humanist public policymaking.

Sometimes it's not enough to seek systemic process as we continue to utilize less-ideal means. For example, though humanists are supportive of reproductive freedom and have compassion for those who decide they can't take care of a recently born child, we don't envision a world where unwanted babies are regularly abandoned to die. Infanticide isn't legal for a number of reasons, but perhaps the most important one is that legalizing it would have the effect of creating a society where killing an innocent independent person was accepted. According to Steven Pinker in *Enlightenment Now: The Case for Reason, Science, Humanism, and Progress,* our planet continues on a relatively steady path toward less violence and greater consideration for individual rights, and a key component of that progress is an expanding shared conviction that violence isn't acceptable. We would do ourselves a disservice by normalizing violence. That said, justice systems should be sophisticated enough to differentiate between infanticide and homicide, as is the case in Canada and the United Kingdom. After all, a woman who ends her newborn's life after an episode of postpartum depression or after a pregnancy brought to term because of poverty or religious prejudice, doesn't deserve to be treated the same as someone who murders an adult for revenge.

Whether or not you're among those who would penalize a late-term abortion but not an early-term one, what we're seeing in these debates is that there aren't always stark choices between right and wrong, but dialectic between ideal and unconscionable—one that is viewed differently by those with different experiences and exposures. The best means of limiting infanticide isn't just making it illegal; it's providing education and access to reproductive services from contraception to abortion.

Can Civil Disobedience Be a Component of Public Policy Work?

When does breaking the law in order to protest it go outside the bounds of acceptable humanist behavior? Some would say that civil disobedience in a civil society is inherently uncivil since there are legal mechanisms (like public policy) to challenge the state. But that suggests a fallacy: that democracy works perfectly and that majorities maintain appropriate consideration for minorities. Rather, tradition, faith, and concentrations of wealth and power lead to situations where the normal channels are not enough to address fundamental rights issues.

For generations humanists have participated in illegal sit-ins, rallies, and marches. Dr. James Farmer, AHA awardee and a mentor of mine, led the Congress on Racial Equality in numerous illegal actions as part of the Freedom Rides in order to seek changes in the law. Before *Roe v. Wade*, AHA awardee Dr. Bill Baird helped thousands of women obtain illegal abortions. AHA awardee Dr. Jack Kevorkian publicized the moral end-of-life choice by illegally assisting with suicides. When North Carolina forbade transgender individuals from using bathrooms that comport with their gender identity, many humanists, including Michael Werner, the president of the AHA's endowment fund, facilitated public efforts to break the law in order to expose its discriminatory nature. Were these actions humanistically unethical because they were illegal? Or, if they were all humanistically ethical, how might we make such a determination?

As Charles Frankel wrote in the *New York Times*, civil disobedience can "shame a majority and make it ask itself just how far it is willing to go, just how seriously it really is committed to defending the status quo." That's why civil disobedience may be utilized as a tactic alongside public policy in order to bring about change. By making the issue a matter of public attention and by using that attention to pressure those with the means to assist, the situation may get at least partially addressed by immediate action from a mayor, governor, president, or other official with the ability to make things happen. The publicity can also boost public policy efforts, demonstrating to legislators that the public demands action.

As an aside, it's worth mentioning that the ability to utilize the media to promote the social good has been undermined in recent years as brazenly biased media sources have gained popularity and power. Venues like Fox News on television, Breitbart on the Internet, *Washington Examiner* in print, and what seems like most radio news outside National Public Radio, allow ultraconservatives to live in an echo chamber that confirms their biases and fails to challenge outdated thinking. Even worse, such media sources can lure those who would otherwise be more mainstream down a path away from progress and toward right-wing extremism.

Even without a receptive media environment, there are other compelling reasons to engage in civil disobedience. Obeying and maintaining unjust laws undermines public confidence in the entire justice system. Again quoting Frankel, "A majority's complacent acquiescence in bad laws can undermine the faith of a minority in the power of democratic methods to rectify manifest evils." How can the public, especially Black and Brown folks, maintain trust in the system when videos that capture police officers unjustly murdering Black Americans are frequent and don't lead to appropriate punishment for the perpetrators?

As demonstrated in Khalil Gibran Muhammad's *The Condemnation of Blackness*, the legal process, crime statistics, and the very way we think of crime in this country is riddled with racist foundations that throw into question much of our justice system (something we'll explore further in chapter 10). It's understandable to be initially misled by the data, after all, even W.E.B. Du Bois fumbled for an explanation of the statistics, assuming they were accurate. As Muhammad noted, Du Bois "believed that crime was a normal result of a vast and sudden change, like that of emancipation." But continuing to abide by such a system when we now have the evidence that it's faulty, suggests a failing of sorts, especially if we don't take part in efforts to correct the existing wrongs.

It's also possible that one's sense of urgency isn't addressed by seeking long-term policy change. Nicholas Guyatt illustrates this in his book *Bind Us Apart*, quoting Henry Knox, the first U.S. Secretary of War, as saying, "I cannot see much prospect of living in tranquility with them [Native Americans] so long as a spirit of land-jobbing prevails [a practice by which settlers squatted on land that treaties indicated were tribal property]—and our frontier-Settlers entertain the opinion that there is not the same crime (or indeed no crime at all) in killing an Indian as in killing a white man." When lives are on the line and the time doesn't seem to be available to pursue justice through legal channels, does that justify illegal options? Perhaps it does, though making such a bold choice to break the law requires accepting the legal consequences as well as the consequences such actions may imbue to the cause itself.

Most civil disobedience activists not only expect to face punishment in the legal system for breaking the law but also anticipate that their punishment will sway public opinion in their favor. That makes sense from a practical point of view. After all, if anybody has a right to break the law without punishment, then it isn't the law. Back in 1964, when protesters to the whites-only pool in St. Augustine, Florida, jumped in and refused to get out, the property owner poured acid into the pool to get them out. This action by the property owner was viewed to be so obscene that it helped garner support for the Civil Rights Act, which passed just barely at the height of the publicity surrounding this protest.

But not every such act of civil disobedience yields the desired results. Going to the opposite end of the political spectrum, consider former county clerk Kim Davis from Kentucky. Defying a Supreme Court decision, Davis refused to issue same-sex couples marriage licenses, saying that she acted "under God's authority." But her civil disobedience backfired as public opinion went against her. Even conservative Sen. Lindsey Graham (R-SC) called on Davis to "comply with the law or resign." Later, the person she denied service to ran in the primary for the chance to defeat her in the general election.

When considering the use of civil disobedience and analyzing its use across the centuries, it's clear that a line is crossed when physical force is resorted to in the pursuit of progress. Violence perpetrated against people is problematic for several reasons. Violent acts are difficult to predict and may physically harm not only those targeted but also the instigators themselves and bystanders. Violence, seen by many as no resort at all, has a good chance of mobilizing the public against one's cause. And violence has the greatest potential among various means to damage the character of those engaged in it. How can we be sure that baser motivations like personal pain, revenge, fame, and the like aren't tipping our internal scales toward making such actions internally defensible? Once an act of violence is already committed, where does it stop? This isn't to say that violence is never justified in history, as we can find or hypothesize scenarios where such a last resort is the best option available, but truly justified violence is undoubtedly rare.

The impact of violent protest can be ambiguous. In *Bind Us Apart*, Guyatt further points out that the Gabriel Revolution and other slave-led rebellions around 1800 "badly damaged the abolitionist cause in Virginia." Virginia was vacillating on its commitment to slavery, so abolitionists tried to argue that such revolts were evidence that "Black people could not be oppressed without consequences" and that "emancipation and education were the only 'effectual security against revolt.'" But these events stirred the fears of leaders in Virginia, who recommitted to slavery and redoubled their efforts to restrict the free Black population. While these leaders might just as easily have cited an absence of rebellion as justification for continuing slavery, this example demonstrates the challenges associated with relying on violent protest in pursuit of equality, even in cases when its use is otherwise fully justifiable.

As Frankel wrote, there must "be some proportion between the importance of the end one desires to attain and the power of the means one employs to attain it." Unless we're defending ourselves or the defenseless from violent acts, this option shouldn't even be on the table. Thinking about it from a perspective of using civil disobedience to bolster public policy efforts, once peaceful protest crosses over to violent actions, the actions cease to be a public policy tool, even if some may employ violence in pursuit of policy changes.

While violence is, by definition, a nonstarter from a humanist public policy standpoint, an uncompromising commitment to an extreme, rigid ideology is cautioned against in the pursuit of public policy changes. Unfettered idealism is terrific in its internal consistency and pure intent, but its chances at achieving results are limited. When one's aims are considered unthinkable by the majority, it's better to find the more palatable interim steps toward those aims and pursue those instead. Unsustainable ideological purism that fails to concede or cooperate with moderates is simply a waste of energy—and a waste of the resources provided by supporters.

An Approach toward Public Policy Progress

What remains in the discussion of how we determine public policy aims and methods?

So far we've looked at this question with a mix of idealism, pursuing the loftiest aims in the most ethical ways, and realism, pursuing courses and methods that help us achieve our ends. In this vein, we act affirmatively on what we have come to know through humanistic thinking. We rely on the scientific method for our accumulation of knowledge and our testing of ideas because it's the method that produces the best results and is constantly open to reexamination. We remember that facts and statistics are always open to interpretation, and we do our best to interpret them fairly and honestly. With the best information on a subject at hand, we consider alternatives and the consequences those alternatives have on real people—not just on ourselves, or our identity groups, but also on all those who can be foreseeably impacted. As we look at such potentialities, we humanistically take extra care to recognize our privileges, endeavor to work past prejudices, and compassionately consider the needs of all. Empathetically putting ourselves in the shoes of others, we seek egalitarian aims in every pursuit.

There are other practical concerns to consider. In practice, public policy work tends to lean heavily on such pragmatism—even in idealistic movements like humanism. As much as we might like to always proactively seek the change we'd like to realize, political realities intervene. We have to ask ourselves, "What issues and strategies hold the best chance for success in the environment we find ourselves?"

If those opposed to humanist values are in key positions in government, the options for advancement are limited. There may be areas of common ground where consensus exists across the political spectrum, such as in the pursuit of international religious liberty, but that won't characterize the bulk of public policy efforts. While we always seek advancement, sometimes the cobbling together of a majority is so obviously unachievable that it makes sense to work on awareness-raising campaigns that are not meant to lead to immediate legislative victories or even sharp movement in the political needle.

Politicians recognize this too. Minority party members, knowing they can't pass their preferred legislation, often embrace such moments as a chance to be ideologically pure and sponsor bills that have no chance of passing but are close to their hearts and publicly demonstrate how far from the majority party they stand. It appeals to their activist bases and financial supporters and sends a message to ideologically aligned organizations. In the case of progressive initiatives in line with humanist principles, a side benefit is that once such legislation has been introduced, it has a better shot at being taken seriously when the political winds eventually shift. Of course, it makes sense to research and approach the politicians most likely to be supportive of your aims. While their past records and statements are indicators, nothing replaces building relationships with them and their staffs so that more can be understood about their true interests. That said, when the political winds are fully aligned with the opposition, there may be times when public policy groups and activists decide to focus on intentional obstructionism and steadfast political resistance.

Everything changes when your political champions hold the reins of power. Such are times to cash in on favors and advance agendas as quickly as possible. But there are often other factors holding back advancement. Seeing themselves in control, knowing they are under heightened scrutiny, and facing resistance from the now-minority party, politicians have a tendency to move toward the middle. As frustrating as this is for activists, it makes sense. Our allied politicians don't want to waste a moment on legislation that can't be passed in the near future, and they only want to include language in bills that they sponsor that won't unnecessarily aggravate the minority party into staunch opposition. So, even when many of our legislators seek compromise and modest incremental advancement, we have to work doubly hard to demonstrate our support and reasoning behind the more transformational change we want to see enacted. If politicians can be convinced they have the support of their constituents and the organizations that will effectively promote shared views in the public square, they can be persuaded to move forward more boldly.

Boldness is something progressives need now more than ever. As Mike Wiley wrote for *AlterNet*, Republicans aggressively pursue their agendas even if they are out of the mainstream, but Democrats "have been so beaten down by the conservative attack machine that they have allowed themselves to get into the habit of being cautious." Sure, such caution prevents possible losses that diminish political capital and may prevent divisions among constituents, but it also ultimately ensures the absence of significant durable progress and reduces enthusiasm among supporters enough to prevent the construction of a lasting progressive power base on Capitol Hill. Instead of being cowed by fear, the times we live in call for an unflinching reproach of the openly racist, sexist, anti-LGBTQ, anti-atheist, anti-immigrant pandering that we're seeing from the ultraconservative Religious Right.

In envisioning the world we want to realize and in developing our progressive approach to policy priorities, we should follow the outlined humanist path that captures the best aims and best methods. A close analysis of the political situation we find ourselves in on any given issue will also suggest what approach we might best take in order to make change happen. Consistently and boldly applying this approach to public policy work, we have the chance at transformational change that can move society forward and, most importantly, not leave anyone behind.

* * *

Recommended Reading

Alfonso Caramazza and Randi C. Martin, "Classification in Well-Defined and Ill-Defined Categories: Evidence for Common Processing Strategies," *Journal of Experimental Psychology* 109, no. 3 (1980): 320–353. www.wjh.harvard.edu/~caram/PDFs/1980_Martin_Caramazza_JEPG.pdf

Nicholas Guyatt, *Bind Us Apart: How Enlightened Americans Invented Racial Segregation* (Basic Books. 2016).

John F Kennedy, "Transcript: JFK's Speech on His Religion," *National Public Radio*, September 12, 1960. www.npr.org/templates/story/story.php?storyId=16920600

Chris Ray, "God's Law vs Man's Law," *Prepared Christian*, July 6, 2012. preparedchristian.net/gods-law-vs-mans-law/#.WljZVainE2w

Liliane Stern, "Abortion Prevents Infanticide in U.S.," *Lancaster Online*, February 20, 2015. lancasteronline.com/opinion/abortion-prevents-infanticide-in-u-s/article_17ed8b58-b6d4-11e4-8465-739536f4f00f.html

United States Senate, "Filibuster and Cloture," January 2018. www.senate.gov/artandhistory/history/common/briefing/Filibuster_Cloture.htm

Mike Wiley, "Progressive Revolution: We Can't Afford to Play Small-Ball and Tip-Toe Around Right-Wingers Anymore," *Alternet*, January 18, 2009. circleof13.blogspot.com/2009/01/progressive-revolution-we-cant-afford.html

Matthew Yglesias, "The Silenced Majority," *Atlantic*, January/February 2009. www.theatlantic.com/magazine/archive/2009/01/the-silenced-majority/307230/

SECTION II
JUSTICE-CENTERED HUMANISM

5

WHY SOCIAL JUSTICE?

* * *

Once prejudice against nontheists fades away, religious favoritism is removed from government, and humanists everywhere are appreciated for their kind and reason-based thinking, then we can begin to focus full-time on promoting our science-based, compassionate, and egalitarian vision for our world. But until that day dawns, we must try to make a difference in as many ways as possible, even if we have not yet realized many of our longstanding goals. To delay action on other fronts, when action could improve lives, would be to negatively impact the fates of many. This isn't an acceptable course.

As humanists become more widely recognized as a group that prizes ethical principles and scientific knowledge, they should use what leverage they have to ensure that human and civil rights are extended to all and not just to a few. If we want a better world, we humans are the only ones to do it. This is an opportunity to matter, to impact the course of history for the better, and to improve the story of humanity.

While many humanists embrace social justice work without hesitation, it's worth mentioning that all aren't on board. Some folks characterize social justice work as a kind of toxic identity politics that narrows perspectives and leaves reason and debate behind. That is a mischaracterization, but it does hint at valid concerns. As journalist He Zhao wrote for *Medium*, "Fundamentalist social justice focuses on calling-out individuals for inadvertently reproducing oppression, on berating and ostracizing them for using offensive words and having wrong opinions, rather than on the understanding and dismantling of oppressive structures which shapes beliefs and behavior." This criticism is somewhat unfair as folks can speak out against racist and sexist language *and* work on structural problems at the same time, but as Zhao continues, some social justice advocates "can be overzealous, dogmatic, and judgmental. Their voices can be shrill, and sometimes become tragically exclusionary (which paradoxically hurts the movement itself); but understandably so: for the first time some victims of oppression have any voice at all."

This isn't surprising really. Beyond those who exercise their right to their oppression-sourced anger, every movement and social group additionally has its own uncompromising, dogmatic individuals who focus more on tearing structures (and people) down than on building a better future for everyone. But the bulk of those who seek social justice are simply seeking fairness for those groups in society that are still getting a bad deal today. They work toward an equal playing field for everyone, an end in which humanists can naturally see value.

For some, it's challenging to evaluate whether social justice–related concerns are rooted in strong foundations or weak dogma, but we perform better if we acknowledge our privileges, set aside explicit biases, do what we can to recognize and overcome implicit biases, and address our own fragility when it comes to self-analysis.

Explicit racism, sexism, and the like are both conscious and overt. They tear at the hearts and minds of humanists and others who embrace egalitarianism. Implicit racism is more subtle, less galvanizing, and can be unconsciously perpetrated, but that doesn't make it any less pernicious. Implicit bias remains hard to change, but new ways to address it are being considered all the time. Implicit biases impact all kinds of judgments from those a jury makes to those a hiring manager makes. (You can test your own implicit biases online with the Harvard implicit bias test at https://implicit.harvard.edu/implicit/takeatest.html.)

Robin DiAngelo, a lecturer at the University of Washington who spoke at the AHA annual conference in 2017, coined the term "white fragility" to address a counterproductive behavior commonly seen in dominant culture. DiAngelo explains,

> White fragility is a state in which even a minimum amount of racial stress becomes intolerable, triggering a range of defensive moves. These moves include the outward display of emotions such as anger, fear, and guilt, and behaviors such as argumentation, silence, and leaving the stress-inducing situation. These behaviors, in turn, function to reinstate white racial equilibrium.

This insight could equally apply to other forms of behavior, such as male fragility, hetero fragility, and the like. Without being confined by attempts to cater to white/male/hetero comfort, it makes sense to seek strategic approaches that are the most persuasive ways of prompting change. As actor Jesse Williams said at the 2016 Black Entertainment Television (BET) awards, "The burden of the brutalized is not to comfort the bystander."

Bringing this issue up is especially important to challenge assumptions about how free we are from the -isms that are all around us in this culture. After all, as I've heard said, though unattributed, "When you're accustomed to living with privilege, equality feels like oppression." In fact, while bigoted speech and action often come before the myths used to justify such actions, we can head-off those actions first, both so that we act better and so that we don't unconsciously reinforce bias in our own thinking. By recognizing our own defensiveness for what it is, we may be able to push past it and better ourselves in ways that help us to better our culture.

Social justice advocacy involves respect for the equality of all people, compassion for their dignity and welfare, and a conviction that positive change requires human intervention. We shouldn't have to struggle to see women and minorities as humans, and thus a natural focus for humanist activism. Ideally, we take an intersectional approach to pursuing social justice. According to *Webster's Dictionary*, intersectionality "refers to the complex and cumulative way that the effects of different forms of discrimination (such as racism, sexism, and classism) combine, overlap, and yes, intersect—especially in the experiences of marginalized people or groups." This fits with our humanist understanding to the point that it's almost foundational to humanism itself. Humanists pursue a way of thinking that we are convinced is more positive and effective, not just for ourselves, but for all in society, particularly marginalized groups.

This can be applied in a number of contexts, such as in addressing the myths of meritocracy. We aren't living in the meritocracy some folks may think this is. We know the accident of where we are born and to what sort of parents we are born dramatically limits our chances or opens doors of opportunity. Inheritance laws, prejudicial advantages, class barriers, glass ceilings, and many other factors also direct us toward success or failure in our endeavors. Without removing personal responsibility for our actions, we will cultivate better empathy and compassion for others in society if we understand that we don't all have the same prospects. Just as the successful don't always necessarily achieve that success on merit, neither do the unsuccessful always necessarily achieve their state due to lack of merit. Recognizing this frames our understanding and need for pursuing social justice.

If these conversations make you feel uncomfortable, embrace it. Feeling uncomfortable and awkward are signs that real internal change is being confronted. There's no reason to feel embarrassed that you have progress to make on social justice issues. We all live in a society where the norms work against us on such topics, so it would be surprising if even the most conscious and enlightened folks didn't still have work to do in some areas. Doing that good work helps us become better allies, and we can strive to be more than just good allies on the periphery who provide only moral support. We can also be good accomplices and co-conspirators with those activists on the front lines. We can stand with them, speak with them, and even risk arrest with them when engaging in civil disobedience for good causes. As University of Baltimore professor emeritus Lenneal Henderson said during a February 2019 Baltimore Ethical Society platform speech, "There's no shame in being who you were. There is shame in failing to evolve from where you are." We're living in a time when our commitment to personal growth and our involvement in collaborations can make a difference.

* * *

Recommended Reading

Robin DiAngelo, "White Fragility," *International Journal of Critical Pedagogy* 3, no. 3 (2011). libjournal.uncg.edu/ijcp/article/view/249

He Zhao, "Social Justice, Identity Politics, and the Liberal Fundamentalism Poisoning It," *Medium*, February 25, 2017. medium.com/@leohezhao/social-justice-identity-politics-and-the-liberal-fundamentalism-poisoning-it-4156a7455988

Ijeoma Oluo, *So You Want to Talk about Race* (Hachette Books, 2018).

Jesse Williams, "Speech on Race at the BET Awards," *Black Entertainment Television*, June 27, 2016. time.com/4383516/jesse-williams-bet-speech-transcript/

6

RACIAL JUSTICE

* * *

Challenging the antiblackness that perpetuates inequality is a tall task, but it's one that humanists must embrace.

Popular notions of white supremacy view it as a form of extremism exclusively embodied by white supremacists in the KKK, Christian Identity, Aryan Nations, and other certified hate groups, but that's just the tip of the iceberg regarding how white supremacy has endured over the generations and continues to impact peoples' lives today.

That white supremacy is supported by more than the fringe groups is intuitive when we give it more than a moment's thought. After all, we can't blame just this tiny group of far-right bigots for the continued nationwide disparities in employment, in housing, in health outcomes, and so forth.

For anyone out there who think the struggle ended with Barack Obama's presidency, I'll just mention that nearly half of all hate crimes in the U.S. are racially motivated. Black men and women are many times more likely than white people to be beaten, raped, or killed by police. Black folks earn 86 cents for every dollar white folks earn, and according to a 2018 Center for American Progress report on systemic inequality, the wealth disparity is much greater: "In 2016, the median wealth for Black and Hispanic families was $17,600 and $20,700, respectively, compared with white families' median wealth of $171,000."

While any area of bias can be explored further to uncover its racist origins and continuing racist impact, let's delve a touch deeper into one area of bias often used to openly justify prejudice. The racial bias entrenched in mass incarceration is a phenomenon with a history and present that is too often overlooked. When statistics, like the incredibly disproportionate number of Black folks behind bars, are touted as an example of continued racial bias, diverse liberals will often express hopelessness about the situation, often viewing crime statistics as if they accurately represented criminal activity, when in fact, they don't.

Khalil Gibran Muhammad's *The Condemnation of Blackness* does a superb job explaining how we got to where we are today regarding our institutionally unfair justice system and the invalid statistics it generates. He takes us back to the very founding of this nation when free Blacks were small in number compared to the many enslaved Blacks who were stolen from their lands and forced into chains. He shows how racism against free Blacks at that time distorted the picture of crime in America. From the beginning of our justice system, innocent Black people were scapegoated by police for crimes they had nothing to do with, while whites were given the benefit of the doubt. Think of *To Kill a Mockingbird* as a storied example of the racism in the system, one in which completely innocent Black men are wrongly convicted for a crime or even killed outright by authorities.

The laws themselves were structured in ways to target those who didn't happen to be white as a method of pushing them out of white neighborhoods and towns. When Black folks sought police intervention for racially motivated violence against them, it was the Black victims who were most likely to be arrested and possibly treated to additional violence at the hands of their presumed protectors. And all that is just the entry point into the justice system. Inferior legal representation awaited them if they were to appear before a judge. Racist juries were likely to convict despite lack of evidence. Racist judges handed out lengthy prison sentences.

In an environment such as this, it can hardly be a surprise to learn that the crime data doesn't yield fair or equal results. All these frequent but false arrests and convictions have long been tracked in crime statistics that many incorrectly presume to be neutral. While unjust policing, convicting, and sentencing continue to this day, the common knowledge of the statistical disparities (public for over a hundred years) also resulted in expectation biases. Since many people assume Black people are more likely to be engaged in criminal activity, they are more likely to "see" such activity, even if it's not there, and act on it, perpetuating the problem even more. In the end, how can we say Black people commit more crime in this country when the data is based on a myriad of prejudiced factors? We can't. Or at least we shouldn't draw conclusions from such suspect source material.

Some folks might tell me, "That's ancient history; things are different today." But how different are they really? As noted in a July 2017 Drug Policy Alliance report, government survey data in New York City show that a greater percentage of whites use marijuana as compared to Blacks and Latinos, a disparity in usage that has existed for years. But their report also shows that only 14 percent of arrests for marijuana possession were white. This displays the disparate effect some laws have on groups targeted for discrimination in this country. Black Americans face selective enforcement, selective prosecution, and selective sentencing—where "selective" can be replaced with "racist."

Racism isn't anywhere near being over. In fact, white supremacy can continue indefinitely even when white supremacists are a thing of the past, and that's because, after hundreds of years, antiblackness has become structural and institutional.

Structural and Institutional Racism

I was fortunate to participate in a class taught at AHA headquarters in 2018 by Dr. William Hart, a professor at Macalester College who researches the intersection of religion, ethics, and politics. Dr. Hart explained how historical, cultural, institutional, and personal practices systematically advantage white people and disadvantage Black people and other racialized groups. Government entities, employers, churches, and schools have racially biased laws, policies, and practices that advantage white people in our society. Such bias is reinforced in popular culture by racially prejudiced portrayals online, in television, and at the movies.

While we can intuit that explicit racism is especially common in many localities, just looking at the federal government alone, there's a record of actions that provide the historical framework for how we got to where we are now. Blatant racial bias was apparent beginning with the founding of our nation and the U.S. Constitution's three-fifths clause, which helped determine the number of members of Congress that came from a given state. One hundred percent of the white people living in a state plus three-fifths of the slaves living there counted toward the total used for the allocation of U.S. representatives. A few years later, the 1790 Naturalization Act permitted only free white immigrants to become full citizens. During the years of slavery, a plethora of laws and economic machinations entrenched inequality.

As Edward E. Baptist writes in *The Half Has Never Been Told*,

> Enslaved people recognized that the slavery they were experiencing was shaped by the ability of whites to move African Americans' bodies wherever they wanted. Forced migration created markets that allowed whites to extract profit from human beings. It brought about a kind of isolation that permitted enslavers to use torture to extract new kinds of labor. It led to disease, hunger, and other kinds of deadly privations. So as these vernacular historians tried to make sense of their own battered lives, the word "stole" became the core of a story that explained.

Baptist went on to describe something that was entirely new to me in its inhumanity. The South, bent on maintaining and expanding slavery, took every opportunity to do just that. Recognizing that their greatest wealth was not in land or goods but in Black bodies, during an economic downturn they literally mortgaged slaves and sold bonds based on those mortgages in order to fund the continuation and expansion of slavery. Investors in the North on Wall Street and around the world profited as slaves worked to pay off their owners' mortgages. Baptist explains,

This meant that investors around the world would share in revenues made by hands in the field. Thus, in effect, even as Britain was liberating the slaves of its empire, a British bank could now sell an investor a completely commodified slave: not a particular individual who could die or run away, but a bond that was the right to a one-slave-sized slice of a pie made from the income of thousands of slaves.

This, by the way, further dispels the myth that the North somehow didn't benefit from slavery or share the blame for its persistence—the North also gained from all the inexpensive raw material (cotton and other products) for the garment and other manufacturing districts in Northern cities.

If these lessons seem lost in antiquity, consider this: some of the same and successor firms on Wall Street that invested in slave mortgages also spurred the subprime mortgage crisis that began in 2007. These firms benefited from bailouts while nearly half the entire wealth of African Americans was lost. A 2014 Pew report indicates that median net worth of Black households decreased 43 percent from 2007 to 2013—perhaps the most significant loss of Black wealth since being stolen into the institution of slavery itself.

Entangled in racism against Black Americans is the racism against Native Americans. With that in mind it's worth recalling the 1830 Indian Removal Act that stole native lands and forced the relocation of Cherokee, Creek, and other Indian nations West of the Mississippi River. The 1862 Homestead Act incentivized further intrusion of whites into native lands and established a base of white wealth that would last generations by distributing hundreds of millions of acres of land to whites for modest filing fees. Despite rampant violations of those treaties by the United States, actual nation-to-nation communication has remained consistent through today. In modern struggles for native and indigenous rights, innovative ideas are being explored, such as a land tax of sorts being levied on a city, or other jurisdiction, for the rent that ought to be due for settler use of the lands. Education, exposure, and accountability are key to these various reform efforts.

During the New Deal era, there were breakthroughs in the national discourse on racism that began to raise awareness. Though the improvement in rhetoric was notable, and some substantive gains were evident in the hundreds of thousands of African Americans employed in government works, this was unfortunately still an era of building walls, not tearing them down. As Jim Powell, a senior fellow at the Cato Institute, pointed out, the regulations against employing unskilled labor resulted in half a million Blacks losing their jobs. Cutting farm production to force up food prices resulted in fewer farm jobs and higher costs of living. The initial provisions of the Wagner Act and the Aid to Families with Dependent Children allowed for federal oversight prohibiting racial discrimination, but that was dropped, opening the door to rampant discrimination. The bulk of New Deal spending was directed away from Black communities by focusing it in the West, authorizing separate and lower payscales for Black people, and (as with the Social Security Act) excluding most job categories (such as domestic and agricultural work) traditionally filled by Black people.

Later legislation continued the tactics of previous efforts to discriminate against the Black community. The GI Bill, for instance, excluded most Black veterans because they were disqualified by zoning rules and individual racism from buying homes in most white neighborhoods, and banks simply wouldn't grant mortgages in Black neighborhoods.

During Reconstruction and the Jim Crow era in the South, state and local laws enforced segregation and ensured that separate was extremely unequal, specifying more funding and better resources for whites. The harshness of these laws was brought home to me on a visit to Little Rock, Arkansas, where I had a tour of Central High School, once considered one of the best high schools in the nation. It was an impressive establishment that clearly benefited from generous funding and received all the best from the beginning. There was a clear contrast between Central High, which was whites-only before the *Brown v. Board of Education* decision, and the dramatically less-funded Horace Mann High School, which was reserved for Black students at the time.

On this tour I learned how the Little Rock Nine came to be the students to test school desegregation. When word went out to the over five hundred Black students living within the area of Central High, over eighty were brave enough to express interest and participate in an arduous series of interviews that questioned their academic preparation for the school and emotional and physical readiness for the certain bullying to come. Our exceptional tour guide had us walk the walk of Elizabeth Eckford, who arrived alone her first day and faced a mob of hundreds of angry white people. As this fifteen-year-old girl walked toward the school, more and more people came at her, hurling the meanest insults they could think up, brandishing confederate flags and signs with messages like "Go Back to Africa Negroes." The new dress she helped make for that first day of school was soaked from all the saliva spit at her by the crowd. Under orders of the governor, the National Guard in attendance turned her away from the school, and she had to make her way further through the crowd to a bus stop as they threatened to rape and lynch her.

As a parent of a daughter the same age at the time I took the tour, I was overwhelmed with sadness for the plight of Eckford and her fellow students, and I felt a deep-seated wrath for the bigoted crowd and all who supported the hateful segregation. As we sat in the auditorium at Central High, the knowledgeable guide told us some of the details of the bullying, starting with what happened in that very auditorium when the lights were dimmed for events. It went beyond threats and other verbal abuse to being pushed down stairs, poked with tacks, and hit in the head with padlocks. I could only imagine how parents of those nine kids had to struggle every moment of the time their kids attended Central High, knowing that their sons and daughters were struggling constantly and that their very lives were always at risk.

When I've spoken with even rather progressive (white) folks, I've observed a tendency for people to bemoan the state of inequality but say something to the effect that "there's no issue here for me since I'm not a racist," but it's not so simple. It's essentially impossible for whites not to benefit from racist structures and institutions that are all around us in society. When you're favored for housing, hiring, car buying, and a whole slew of other life experiences, it's rarely even an option to deny that favoritism.

These privileges reveal themselves in significant ways all the time. As a tall white cisgender straight man, if I'm pulled over by a police car in rural America, I only have to worry about paying a ticket, not potentially being arrested, beaten, or killed. That's a privilege Black and Brown folks don't have. I don't have to train my white daughters to avoid carrying toy guns, lest they be shot by racially biased police or security guards. I can easily choose to be around people who won't distrust me on sight. I'll be seen as credible if I report that there is (or isn't) an issue of racial bias at hand.

Sometimes even when discrimination is unknown or uncertain, it impacts lives just the same. As a white man, I can almost always assume I'm not being treated badly because of the color of my skin. I can only imagine what it would be like to wonder whether race was a factor if I got rejected for a home loan or apartment offer, got quoted an overly high price for a new car, or missed out on a job opportunity.

Working actively to combat prejudice in everything we do and constantly questioning simple everyday privileges is an important step, but that doesn't erase the historic momentum and massively pervasive white supremacy in which we find ourselves.

When thinking about our individual collective role in perpetuating white supremacy, we can occupy any one of a number of possible spaces, from blatant bigot to fully woke. To simplify, consider the below five categories:

- Blatant bigot: Hate-group members with explicit bias

- Willfully ignorant: Advantage takers who deny their privilege and deny white supremacy

- Uninformed: Well-meaning people who aren't aware of how they regularly contribute to racism

- Partially informed: Do-gooders who have sought information about antiracism but may have stopped their efforts too soon

- Fully woke: Elusive activists who are consciously antiracist but whose learning and understanding constantly needs updating

Where do you stand in the above hierarchy? I ask not to make us feel better by putting ourselves in a good category. Nor to get us off the hook from having to educate ourselves. Nor as an alternative to working for change. Humanism can't alleviate racism without education, de-learning, and active work toward racial equity. Advantages to explaining this playing field is that it can help communicate understanding, and from there it can encourage folks to move toward more productive positions. It's helpful as long as we remember that no matter where we might be today, we have more to do for the foreseeable future.

Even though few would self-identify as belonging to the first or perhaps even second category, we should self-examine as best as we can as a precursor to betterment. This same exercise could also apply to other -isms. The partially informed are common among humanist elders who were active in earlier civil rights movements but who aren't up to speed on how they can best help now. I put myself in that category from time to time as it takes work to stay informed and to participate in pursuing justice. During and after college I decided I'd read enough of the straight white male canon and focused on reading and listening to as many other sources as I could. I participated in trainings, I trained to become a trainer, and I co-led different types of diversity trainings for hundreds of people. But over time I realized it takes a lifetime of learning to become more and more woke and not fall behind the times, as new historical and activist scholarship becomes available. We must be attentive to direct sources, be careful to avoid erasure, and be ever cognizant of the difference between intention and impact.

It's worth noting that even the woke live and breathe in a bigoted world. We've all been exposed to a lifetime of socialization that subtly and not so subtly influences our thoughts. Being an antiracist means being on the alert and doing our best to overcome this.

What's more, whiteness is the default in our culture; it is the unmentioned norm. Like implicit bias, we generally unconsciously assume white, which is why you'd have a hard time finding headlines that read, "Whites Win Big at the Oscars" or "White Mother of Four Wins Lottery." Racial references aren't needed since it's normalized.

When white men commit atrocities (like the Las Vegas shooter or the Oklahoma City bomber), the media rarely mention their race or religion. That's not so when the perpetrator happens to be Black, Muslim, or both. This, in turn, leads to dehumanization. Black folks are holders of race in our culture in a way that suggests they are second-class citizens at best and inhuman at worst. Since even humanist circles aren't immune from the white default, extra effort is needed to remove humanism from white supremacist structures. This includes making the American Humanist Association a decidedly antiracist institution.

Such a course certainly fits with humanism's embrace of science. To perceive difference is natural. But to construct a hierarchy of people based on arbitrary attributes is antiscientific and nonhumanist. So let's embrace our responsibility to challenge antiblackness.

A New Reconstruction

As we consider the overwhelming task of making right the multitude of wrongs perpetrated for generations against African Americans, a bold approach is needed, perhaps a newer, better reconstruction era.

In a piece for CNN titled, "Is Black Lives Matter Blowing It?" John Blake points out the importance of learning from past movements, explaining that while the participants in the Occupy Wall Street movement had their noteworthy successes, they are no longer players in the debate. He cites historian Jerald E. Podair, who said, "They did not adapt. They were so protest- and spectacle-oriented that they never made the transition into electoral politics, which is where the power is in a democracy." While on the whole Blake and others are too critical in their concerns about Black Lives Matter not being adaptable or policy focused, such criticism does point to the importance of finding ways to work within the system if we want the system to change.

The Black Lives Matter movement began with the hashtag highlighting the police brutality and the unjust 2013 acquittal of George Zimmerman in his killing of teen Trayvon Martin. The movement gained steam as videos of white police perpetrating violence against Black citizens became more accessible and frequent. Today, police oversight is still desperately needed and is a unifying element for the movement.

After the unarmed Michael Brown was shot to death in Ferguson, Missouri, the U.S. Department of Justice launched an investigation into the city's police department. As reported in the *Atlantic* by Conor Friedersdorf, they discovered that the "Ferguson officials leeched off the Black community as shamelessly as would mafia bosses." They established a system to catch nearly everyone for some kind of infraction, allowing the police to target communities as their bias directed. At the time of the report, an astounding 16,000 people (of the 21,000 residents of Ferguson) had outstanding arrest warrants, and 96 percent of the arrests for outstanding warrants were African American. As part of a package of reform measures, President Obama established a task force to investigate other police departments across the nation, but when Trump became president, the task force was quickly brought to a halt. What's needed is a much more comprehensive investigation and ongoing oversight in order to ensure that those who are sworn to protect us aren't working against us.

But even if racism in law enforcement was completely addressed, many problems would remain. We need to inspire energy and fortitude to address the full breadth of antiblackness today. Multiple problems must be addressed simultaneously, since they build on one another. What's needed to eliminate structural and institutional white supremacy?

I've spoken to a number of well-meaning white folks who are concerned that they hear anger and dismay from the Black community (all completely understandable emotions), but not specific advice as to what needs to be done and how. Of course, it's not the job of the oppressed to educate their oppressors, but for those who really want the information and aren't just complaining about the anger to excuse themselves from participating in a solution, recommendations are not hard to find. The Movement for Black Lives (M4BL), for example, offers a platform called "Vision for Black Lives" for addressing the myriad of issues before us, and much can be gained from reviewing and implementing many of its cultural aims and traditional policy recommendations.

While the organization's platform has been maligned as extreme or impractical by critics, on reading it you'll discover how well-designed, reasonable, and practical it is. The original 2016 platform (since updated in 2020) reads, "We understand that policy change is one of many tactics necessary to move us towards the world we envision." The 2016 platform also contains the following six broad demands, which are not really so radical. Each of the six demands offers several solutions that address the topic, and each of those solutions are linked to specific actions, recommended policy, and even model legislation that can help achieve them. Whether or not you agree with each and every one of the demands or proposed solutions, you likely agree with most, and after reading them you'll know of a number of ways you can help make a difference. Here are their six top-level original demands, plus my summaries about how they are connected to policy change.

"We demand an end to the named and unnamed wars on Black people—including the criminalization, incarceration, and killing of our people." Humanists can certainly get behind the detailed points within this category, from ending the death penalty, stopping "defendant-funded" court proceedings, and removing zero-tolerance policies, to stopping the use of solitary confinement, addressing physical sexual abuse in prisons, and adding queer and gender-nonconforming people to antidiscrimination civil rights protections.

"We demand reparations for harms inflicted on Black people; from colonialism to slavery through food and housing redlining, mass incarceration, and surveillance." Although this is possibly the most controversial of the top-level demands, the required funding is arguably a bargain in addressing the extreme financial bad deal laid at the feet of Black Americans—it begins with support for H.R. 40, the "Commission to Study Reparation Proposals for African Americans Act," or subsequent versions that call for reparations remedies.

"We demand investments in the education, health, and safety of Black people, instead of investments in the criminalizing, caging, and harming of Black people." Since studies show that jobs and education make communities stronger and keep them safer, this invest-divest strategy calls for reinvestment of federal grants from policing and incarceration to education, employment, and other services in Black communities most impacted by mass incarceration and crime. It also calls for universal health care, free higher education, and decriminalizing drugs in ways that humanists are already on record supporting. It also seeks to decriminalize sex work, which may be more controversial in some circles.

"We demand economic justice for all and a reconstruction of the economy to ensure Black communities have collective ownership, not merely access." With the income gap steadily increasing year after year between the richest and the rest of us, even more economically conservative humanists may appreciate the need to correct our supposedly progressive taxation system that is made regressive from a myriad of loopholes and special payouts to the wealthy. Humanists can also get behind increased regulatory protections for domestic workers, farm workers, and tipped workers, as well as support for co-ops and social economy networks. Some humanists might also support renegotiating trade agreements to prioritize workers and communities, breaking-up the large banks, and gaining democratic control over how environmental resources are preserved, used, and distributed.

"We demand a world where those most impacted in our communities control the laws, institutions, and policies that are meant to serve us." By adopting civilian oversight boards and ensuring they have the powers needed to act, violence can be reduced and the communities supported. Importantly, they must be able to create transparency by obtaining means of retrieving information, including subpoena power. Such civilian agencies would also be given the ability to hire and fire officers, determine

discipline, determine funding, and enforce policies. This demand also seeks to change the budget process at all levels so it begins with the needs of communities, and emphasizes those suffering from injustice, and then raises revenue in an equitable way to fund needs-based budgets. Along those lines, there's a need for more government involvement in the expansion of affordable housing in order to overcome the lack of peak-market reasons for building housing accessible to lower-income people. Government must take the lead subsidizing tenants, incentivizing landlords, and using regulations to require large developers to include affordable housing.

"We demand full and independent Black political power and Black self-determination in all areas of society." This demand can be met, in part, through the public financing of elections and the elimination of super PACs and unchecked corporate donations, two goals already identified by humanist organizations. It also humanistically seeks universal, automatic voter registration, and a ban on any disenfranchisement laws. Additionally, it calls for an end to the tradition of government surveillance, harassment, and imprisonment of political activists and those in freedom movements. It demands protection and increased support for Black institutions.

Some humanists will likely object to the platform's more socialist-oriented economic elements, even though this type of approach is understandable given the ultimate aims of the platform. For example, it would be hard to envision achieving the same goals without government regulation and a conscious decision to have an economic focus on people and communities. How humanists can approach this aspect is something we'll be looking at later in chapter 11.

Other humanists may view recommendations like reparations as being beyond the scope of what might possibility be implemented in the foreseeable future. Indeed, while reparations for the comparatively small number of individuals impacted by the Japanese internment camps were a successful and positive step, doing so for the descendants of slaves would be much more complicated, expensive, and politically challenging to implement. According to a 2016 AP survey, there are very few groups polling in support of reparations, with only 58 percent of Black people supporting the idea. With a slim majority of millennials supportive of reparations, this goal may become more feasible over time.

Morally, it's difficult to have an issue with reparations. Some argue that slavery is long past and that its impact is no longer felt, but as Ta-Nehisi Coates successfully argued in his *Atlantic* article titled "The Case for Reparations," the financial harm inflicted on African Americans during slavery isn't the only harm requiring rectification; more recent harm must be addressed too. As Coates explained, during and even after Reconstruction, "In the Deep South, a second slavery ruled. In the North, legislatures, mayors, civic associations, banks, and citizens all colluded to pin Black people into ghettos, where they were overcrowded, overcharged, and undereducated."

Some will no doubt criticize the M4BL platform for its narrow point regarding how the United States has worked with Israel on its global war on terror, calling Israel an apartheid state that is complicit with genocide. While I'm sympathetic to such concerns about the platform, anything as far-reaching as the M4BL platform is likely to have elements we can't all fully embrace. This shouldn't be held as a barrier to progress and wouldn't prevent me from assisting to achieve the other goals of the platform, and I hope others would take a similar approach.

As we move on to other policy topics, keep in mind that a number of ideas expressed in this section can be applied to other forms of prejudice and discrimination.

* * *

Recommended Reading

Edward E. Baptist, *The Half Has Never Been Told* (Basic Books, 2016).

John Blake, "Is Black Lives Matter Blowing It?" CNN, August 2, 2026. www.cnn.com/2016/07/29/us/black-lives-matter-blowing-it/

Ta-Nehisi Coates, "The Case for Reparations," *Atlantic*, June 2014. www.theatlantic.com/magazine/archive/2014/06/the-case-for-reparations/361631/

Angela Hanks, Danyelle Solomon, and Christian E. Weller, "Systemic Inequality," Center or American Progress, February 21, 2018. www.americanprogress.org/issues/race/reports/2018/02/21/447051/systematic-inequality/

Jesse J Holland, "Poll: Millennials More Open to Idea of Slavery Reparations," Associated Press, May 11, 2016. apnews.com/b183a022831d4748963fc8807c204b08/poll-millennials-more-open-idea-slavery-reparations

Rakesh Kochhar and Richard Fry, "Wealth Inequality Has Widened along Racial, Ethnic Lines Since End of Great Recession," Pew Research Center, December 12, 2014. www.pewresearch.org/fact-tank/2014/12/12/racial-wealth-gaps-great-recession/

Movement for Black Lives, "Vision for Black Lives," 2020. m4bl.org/policy-platforms/

Khalil Gibran Muhammad, *The Condemnation of Blackness* (Harvard University Press, 2019).

The White House, Office of the Press Secretary, "Creating Opportunity for All Through Stronger, Safer Communities," Fact Sheet, May 18, 2015. obamawhitehouse.archives.gov/the-press-office/2015/05/18/fact-sheet-creating-opportunity-all-through-stronger-safer-communities

7

GENDER JUSTICE

* * *

The quest for gender justice in the United States is hundreds of years in the making. Progress hasn't been universal or consistent; the push for gender equality has been met with resistance and endured numerous backlashes, but previous gains suggest that continued organizing and involvement in politics is well worth the effort. Our work, our votes, and our participation in the political process matter. As Gloria Steinem once said, "I never wanted to be a politician or elected person myself, so I loved to work for other women who did. . . . The problem is the feeling that we're divided from politics, that our vote doesn't count or what we do doesn't count. In fact, everything we do counts."

The United Nations Development Fund for Women produces a biennial investigation of progress made toward a world where women live free from violence, poverty, and inequality called "Progress of the World's Women." It details how the change in women's share of paid employment in industry and services has increased in a majority of nations over time. It also shows how the ratio of females to males obtaining secondary education is evening out around the world. Critically, it tracks the progress of women's increasing share of seats in representative governments—only a relatively small number of nations, such as Mongolia, Cuba, and Romania, have seen steady declines among general global advancement.

Consider the major advances for women's rights that have been made in the United States. Some aren't aware that there was a time when women not only didn't have the right to vote in U.S. elections (added nationally in 1920), but also didn't have the right to own property in their own name. Even after women gained this right in 1839, they still needed permission from their husbands to own property, and it wasn't until 1981 that the Supreme Court overturned state laws designating a husband "head and master" with unilateral control over property owned jointly with his wife.

Even though female federal employees were officially guaranteed equal pay for equal work under the law in 1872, it wasn't until nearly a hundred years later when the Equal Pay Act officially extended that right to the private sector—including protections for race, color, religion, and national origin. Even then, there was little recourse for those who had been discriminated against, as was made clear in the 2007 Supreme Court decision *Ledbetter v. Goodyear*, which denied Lilly Ledbetter's right to sue for clear wage discrimination. Justice Ruth Bader Ginsburg's dissent in that case laid the groundwork for progress, and in 2009 the Lilly Ledbetter Fair Pay Restoration Act was made law, allowing victims of pay discrimination, most frequently women, to file a complaint with the government against their employer.

Justice Ginsburg, who was so instrumental in advancing rights for women, explained in a 2016 MSNBC interview what progress has been made and the primary challenge that remains:

Our goal in the '70s was to end the closed-door era. There were so many things that were off-limits to women: policing, firefighting, mining, piloting planes. All those barriers are gone. And the stereotypical view of people of a world divided between home and child-caring women and men as breadwinners, men representing the family outside the home, those stereotypes are gone. So we speak of parent rather than mother and wage earner rather than male breadwinner. That job was an important first step. What's left, what's still with us and harder to deal with is what I call unconscious bias.

Even still, the Equal Rights Amendment remains unratified. That straightforward and concise constitutional amendment originally conceived of and introduced in 1921, and reintroduced in 1971, reads:

Section 1. Equality of rights under the law shall not be denied or abridged by the United States or by any state on account of sex.

Section 2. The Congress shall have the power to enforce, by appropriate legislation, the provisions of this article.

Section 3. This amendment shall take effect two years after the date of ratification.

The amendment never passed the required number of state legislatures (three-quarters of states), though in 2017 two additional states ratified it, leaving it one short of passing if certain passage-deadline hurdles can be overcome.

The Expectation of Maleness and Invisibility

Just as whiteness is the assumed default in our culture, so too are men the assumed default when it comes to leadership roles. Thus, women are generally the bearers of gender, whereby gender is noted only if the subject is a woman. The male norm for leadership roles in our society is so pervasive that it's news when women become CEOs, presidents, and even officers at average-sized businesses. This is why we never see headlines that read, for example, "Apple Chooses Man as New CEO," because it's what we'd expect to happen anyway.

As women age, our culture imbues an additional layer of invisibility upon them. Since women are too often seen as merely sex objects, every wrinkle and gray strand of hair suggests to some that they are no longer worth society's attention. As feminist writer Fatema Mernissi wrote for the *New York Times*, "The Western man declares that in order to be beautiful, a woman must look 14-years-old. If she dares to look 50, or worse, 60, she is beyond the pale. By putting the spotlight on the female child and framing her as the ideal of beauty, he condemns the mature woman to invisibility."

A significant portion of work done by women is invisible. According to Gillian White, writing for the *Atlantic*, "The UN finds women do three out of every four hours of unpaid labor, while men do two-thirds of work that is paid." Whether working in informal jobs, childcare, or domestic tasks, women disproportionately carry the burden of performing unpaid, underpaid, and underappreciated work.

These challenges point out how unhealthy expectations of men contribute toward problems for everyone. Male stereotypes are an important aspect of the persistence of gender discrimination, as humanist writer Greta Christina notes: "The willingness to, as my friend Michael put it, 'actually, physically, with fists or other weapons, fight'—to defend one's honor (or the honor of one's lady, or country, or sports team, or whatever)—is more central to how men are taught to see manhood than I had any notion of." The constant acculturation needed to yield such a result doubtlessly also results in heightened aggressiveness. It doesn't take many leaps of logic to see how that could also lead to uncalled-for decisions to use force in many situations, from the intimacy of the home to the world stage.

As Christina further notes, other male stereotypes are similarly problematic, such as the one that says men are supposed to be ready and willing to have sex with anyone (of the "right" gender) at any time—a norm that may be exacerbating gang rape and other sexual violence. For example, the perpetrator of the 2014 Isla Vista, California, killings cited "retribution" as his motivating factor for what can best be described as a misogynist rampage. In his final YouTube video, he says, "Tomorrow is the day of retribution, the day in which I will have my revenge. . . . You girls aren't attracted to me, but I will punish you all for it. I'll take great pleasure in slaughtering all of you. You will finally see that I am in truth the superior one, the true alpha male."

While women undeniably suffer the brunt of sexism, it negatively impacts everyone. For example, while expectations that men deny their emotions (other than desire and anger) and be a family's main breadwinner are bad for men, they also contribute to ongoing sexism and gender discrimination against women.

Violence and Religious Patriarchy

Violence against women is arguably more pervasive than violence against any other category of people. Not surprisingly, among women, women of color face the highest rates of violence. The World Health Organization (WHO) indicated in 2017 that "about 1 in 3 (35 percent) of women worldwide have experienced either physical and/or sexual intimate partner violence or non-partner sexual violence in their lifetime" and that "38 percent of murders of women are committed by a male intimate partner." According to a 2015 National Sexual Violence Resource Center report, rape in the United States is the most underreported crime, with 63 percent of sexual assaults going unreported to police. Further, one in five women will be raped at some point in their lives, and in 80 percent of rape cases, the rapist is known to the victim. While violence and sexual assault of men isn't a problem to be ignored (one in seventy-one men will be raped at some point in their lives), the numbers are objectively clear: the vast majority of perpetrators of rape are men, and the vast majority of the targets for such violence are women.

The WHO offers some substantive metrics that suggest ways to improve the situation and reduce violence against women by men. They found that the probability for men to perpetrate violence increases if they have "low education, a history of child maltreatment, exposure to domestic violence against their mothers, harmful use of alcohol . . . and a sense of entitlement over women." The WHO recommends advocacy and empowerment-counselling interventions, as well as home visitations, to reduce intimate-partner violence against women. Undeniably, education on such topics is of value for boys and girls, women and men, and those who are nonbinary or in transition.

Just as there are steps that might improve the situation, there are steps that can exacerbate it, like the ones that were pushed by President Trump and his Religious Right allies. As president, Trump belittled the appearance of women reporters, actors, and politicians. He mocked the #MeToo movement against sexual harassment and assault, and tried to diminish women's rights activism. While Trump's boast about grabbing women "by the pussy" and the charges of sexual misconduct and assault against him have also been widely reported, less-often discussed are the specific policies he enacted that are detrimental to woman. For example, Trump signed legislation making it harder for women in developing countries to get birth control and reinstated the "Global Gag Rule" that disallows U.S. aid recipients from providing abortion services, information, or even referrals, whether or not they are using such aid to fund that type of work. He signed a bill removing Title X funding for domestic reproductive health education and services. And as Nancy LeTourneau wrote about the Trump Administration for *Washington Monthly*, "in the process of attempting to stop the flow of Black and Brown immigrants, they have instituted policies that pose a threat to women and children, making them sexist as well as racist." And, of course, the Trump Administration pushed for special rights for religious people and companies to discriminate based on their beliefs against women, LGBTQ people, and others.

Appearing on *The Rachel Maddow Show* in 2017, Hillary Clinton stated that Trump's degrading attacks on women lifted the top off previous restraint and that "he gave permission for people to be much more sexist and misogynistic, which is a much more generalized hatred of women." She also explained how Trump and his allies emphasized the kind of things that get in the way of women candidates being taken seriously, including a hyperfocus on appearance, personal family, and day-to-day life.

As an encouraging side note in the midst of this barrage, there was evidence that Trump's conservative extremism had a positive reaction of sorts, as those on the left and in the middle protested in record numbers. According to the *Washington Post*, the Women's March on January 21, 2017, was likely the largest day of demonstrations in U.S. history, with well over three million people participating in the United States, perhaps more than five million. Further, according to CNN, Democratic women are running for office and winning in record-breaking numbers. The influx isn't likely to fade soon. After Trump took office, Emily's List, an organization that supports pro-choice women candidates, saw a twenty-fold increase in the number of women contacting them for election support.

Of course, Trump was not the only problem. Vice President Mike

Pence and numerous right-wing high-level appointments presented challenges for gender justice. They didn't get into office without the support of a far-right faith-based constituency. Indeed, conservative religious organizations who hold patriarchal views seek to legislate their own sectarian antiwoman thinking. We've seen these groups, including the Catholic Church, railing against contraceptive coverage provisions for employers and opposing gender equality, all the while trying to claim that their religious liberty is being limited. The contraceptive-care controversy sheds light on just how far the Religious Right is willing to go to discriminate against women.

In 2010 the U.S. Department of Health and Human Safety issued a rule requiring all employers, except for religious organizations, to cover contraceptive coverage for their employees. Initially, businesses affiliated with religious organizations, but not religious organizations themselves, were also required to provide contraceptive coverage for their employees. However, after significant opposition from religious groups like the U.S. Conference of Catholic Bishops, the Obama Administration compromised and mandated that insurance companies themselves would have to provide contraceptive care to employees of businesses affiliated with religious organizations. While it's nice to know that these employees are getting the vital health services they need, it is upsetting that their employers get a free ride (and that you and I will be subsidizing the expenses of these religiously affiliated businesses). What is even more upsetting is that religious organizations protested this coverage requirement, even though they themselves were never required to provide it and the businesses that are associated with them are off the hook as well. It takes tortured logic to see it from their perspective, but the Christian Right is convinced they have a legal right to discriminate based on their prejudicial religious views. Progressive humanist activists must stand up against such efforts to legislate bigotry.

This war on women really is a battle over values. When the Religious Right advocates for "traditional values," for example, what they mean is that their scriptures are more important than the health or rights of women nationwide. Humanists, freethinkers, and progressive people of faith, on the other hand, value the rights of Americans to necessary health services and to open and nondiscriminatory workplaces.

Given that traditional religion is one of society's greatest props for patriarchy and the disparate treatment of women, it's heartening to know that women are leaving traditional religion in record numbers. According to a 2011 Barna study on religion, women remain more religious than men overall, but women's attendance in church had sunk by 11 percentage points since 1991, Bible reading had plummeted by 10 percentage points, and Sunday school involvement had fallen by 7 points. During the same period, the number of women who were "unchurched" rose 17 percentage points—more than half of American women hadn't attended church once in the previous six months. While religions vary on their commitment to patriarchy, shedding the shackles of gender discrimination in religion is a step in the right direction.

American humanists have an honorable feminist legacy to be proud of, from those who came before us, including the likes of Elizabeth Cady Stanton and Margaret Sanger, to those still active, like Gloria Steinem and Faye Wattleton, to those modern stars of feminism like Jessica Valenti, Malala Yousafzai, and Roxane Gay. Such a legacy can be a great foundation on which to build, but it certainly doesn't mean we've done our part, and it doesn't mean we don't have to continue to educate ourselves and become better feminists. Indeed, nontheism isn't immune from the influences of the broader culture. Female atheists and humanists regularly experience sexist hostility, whether online or in face-to-face gatherings, such as at freethought conferences. Organizations and individuals must address this issue in order to live up to their own words and values.

After all, we need all the advocacy and support we can manage to confront the Religious Right's and its allies' war on women. Bills are regularly introduced by religious political extremists in Congress and the state houses to defund reproductive health services, elevate the rights of a fetus over that of women, repeal equal pay legislation, and more. In this modern era one might think that any form of gender prejudice or discrimination would be widely rejected. However, in addition to the new attacks on women's rights, other forms of institutionalized discrimination continue to plague women, who are often relegated to second-class status by politicians, employers, and even intimate partners. It is essential to step up and guarantee the equality of women in the United States and around the world once and for all.

Today there are many fronts in this struggle that humanists are leading. Humanists have a long history of consistently supporting the Equal Rights Amendment and advocating for its ratification, often against opposition by religious and conservative groups. Now that these same groups and their intellectual offspring are on the offensive again with regard to discrimination against women, humanists and religious allies are determined to see the Equal Rights Amendment finally passed. Interestingly, today, there is another reason to support the amendment. Those on the far right are afraid of its potential power, not only to ensure gender equality in the workplace, but also because its language could help shore-up reproductive rights and extend protections for LGBTQ Americans.

Aside from the Equal Rights Amendment and the Violence Against Women Act, all other efforts meant to level the playing field for women deserve our support.

#MeToo

The #MeToo movement ushered in an opportunity to create positive change. Activist Tarana Burke initially used the phrase "Me Too" in 2006, and then the phrase was popularized in 2017 by actress Alyssa Milano who, utilizing Twitter, said, "If all the women who have been sexually harassed or assaulted wrote 'Me too.' as a status, we might give people a sense of the magnitude of the problem." Inspired by #MeToo, Time's Up launched in January 2018 with celebrity appeal and millions of dollars to work with, issuing the message that there will be "No more silence. No more waiting. No more tolerance for discrimination, harassment, or abuse." The movement clearly delineated what needs to happen, aiming to "improve laws, employment agreements, and corporate policies; help change the face of corporate boardrooms and the C-suite; and enable more women and men to access our legal system to hold wrongdoers accountable."

Time's Up, though facing some criticism for being elitist and celebrity-led, has multiple intriguing ventures. Among them is a collaboration with All Raise, whose mission is to accelerate the success of women funders and founders, seeking to double the number of women partners at sizable tech firms while increasing the percentage of venture funding going to women corporate founders. Time's Up also has a collaboration with Press Forward to address harassment and the need for equal treatment in newsrooms, and it has an advertising initiative to address a whole host of feminist concerns. These modern endeavors, together with the lasting wisdom and activism of groups like the National Organization for Women, Emily's List, and reproductive rights organizations, provide us both hope for the future and guideposts for activism.

It's important not to paint an unrealistically rosy picture of nontheism's past and present, so we must acknowledge that our own movement has been impacted by #MeToo. For example, when multiple allegations of inappropriate behavior were raised against atheist scientist Lawrence Krauss, I said, "When a prominent humanist's commitment to reason, compassion, and egalitarianism appears to be fundamentally compromised by his or her behavior, we must act on our disappointment to ensure that the world understands humanists at large don't condone such misconduct." Krauss was removed from the American Humanist Association's pool of speakers and presenters, and the AHA's Board of Directors, weighing available evidence, decided to withdraw an American Humanist Association award previously given to him. Other science and humanist organizations took similar steps.

Within and without the humanist movement we've seen backlash to progress as purveyors of the old norms have demanded that there be additional consideration and allowances before any public condemnation or organizational distancing from prominent individuals with multiple accusations of inappropriate, and often illegal, behavior. Admittedly, he said, she said situations are sometimes hard to gauge, but how should humanists address such concerns? Let's look to science and reason, and then be guided by compassion and egalitarianism.

The National Sexual Violence Resource Center reports that the prevalence of false reporting for sexual violence is decidedly rare, between 2.1 percent and 7.1 percent, citing three U.S. studies on the subject. A study of eight communities and 2,059 cases of sexual assault found a 7.1 percent rate of false reports. A study of 136 sexual assault cases in Boston found a 5.9 percent rate of false reports. And a study of 812 geographically dispersed reports of sexual assault found a 2.1 percent rate of false reports. Averaging the studies, we're looking at a roughly 95 percent accuracy rate for reported claims. Compare that to CNN, which many people respect as a reliable news source. Politifact rates their truth claims in 2015 as 80 percent true or partially true. Now think about how the likelihood of innocence for the accused drops as multiple independent claims surface. With just two independent claims, it's 97.5 percent likely that they aren't innocent, with three, nearly 99 percent, and with four or more, the chance that they are innocent is virtually zero.

Since this data refers to reports to the police, and we want to know more about the reliability of more generalized public accusations, it's possible the false reporting is higher, especially when the barrier for reporting is lower. But the assumption by some that such reports are wholly unreliable don't take into account the personal risk involved in any kind of reporting. This data and a common-sense review of what reporting such claims entails bolsters the conclusion that claims are not likely to be made unless they have merit.

This suggests we should be taking the accusers at their word, at least when making decisions about matters outside legal proceedings. Such an approach supports our compassionate internal voice, driven by our empathetic concern for those who've suffered harassment, assault, or both. Our compassion for them, as well as our commitment to egalitarianism, directs us to take whatever action we can in support of their claims. For too long women have been asked to adapt to a "man's world," but we know that asking this is wrong. As Gloria Steinem says, "Don't think about making women fit the world—think about making the world fit women."

A Better Future

As we envision a better future where someone's gender isn't a factor in whether they will achieve success in work and life, we must work toward that vision, recognizing that it won't happen overnight. Education is a key component going forward. We need to teach youth about consent and healthy sexual relationships. We need to teach adults about reproductive health, gender-neutral parenting, legal awareness, and appropriate boundaries for workplaces, conferences, and other public settings. And finally, we need to direct a spotlight toward the Religious Right, and expose the underhanded tactics through which they intentionally mislead the public, whether that be through their dubiously named "pregnancy crisis centers," or their efforts to hide their bigotry behind the veil of religious privilege.

The debate over antiabortion religious pregnancy crisis centers provides an instructive example. California joined Hawaii and Illinois in attempting to address this after the California legislature found that these centers "pose as full-service women's health clinics, but aim to discourage and prevent women from seeking abortions," citing their "intentionally deceptive advertising and counseling practices that often confuse, misinform and even intimidate women from making fully informed, time-sensitive decisions." They enacted a law that simply required the antiabortion crisis pregnancy centers to post notices pointing out the existence of publicly funded family-planning services. The centers sued.

While the Supreme Court struck down the law in June 2018, considering the "forced speech" to be a First Amendment violation, the ruling opened up an avenue to challenge antiabortion laws in other states—for example, state laws that compel doctors to convince women not to abort. As Callie Beusman reported for *Broadly* in 2016, thirty-seven states have an "abortion-specific informed consent law in place that requires doctors to counsel patients before the procedure, using information chosen by legislators; in 28 states, women must then reflect for a certain amount of time—usually 24 hours, although some states mandate up to three days—before actually getting the abortion procedure."

Our political advocacy work must address women's economic inequality, legal disadvantages, and sexual and reproductive barriers to equality. We should seek cultural independence, safety and security, and sexual freedom, and ensure equal access to opportunity. To do so, we must be willing to cross barriers, including religious ones, so that we can educate the largest number of people possible and build the critical mass needed to impact the political process in a feminist direction. This also means looking at feminism and other rights struggles through an intersectional lens so we don't miss opportunities to collaborate and advance our shared agendas.

We must also understand that we sometimes do the most good by following instead of leading. We should deepen involvement of women from diverse backgrounds in advocating for, and achieving, women's rights. This can be part of a series of aims we can collectively consider "gender mainstreaming." As Oxfam described it in 2018, this includes "gender justice considerations being built into all stages of a program. This includes integrating strong gender and power analysis, explicit gender justice and women's rights objectives and specific actions to address structural gender discrimination, not just its symptoms." It's essential that we help people see the value in addressing these concerns in every facet of their work and life, and together different aspects of that work will complement each other and allow for the greatest collective impact.

* * *

Recommended Reading

Callie Beusman, "A State-by-State List of the Lies Abortion Doctors Are Forced to Tell Women," *Broadly*, August 18, 2016. broadly. vice.com/en_us/article/nz88gx/a-state-by-state-list-of-the-lies-abortion-doctors-are-forced-to-tell-women

Irin Carmon, "Exclusive Justice Ruth Bader Ginsburg Interview," MSNBC, February 17, 2016. www.msnbc.com/msnbc/exclusive-justice-ruth-bader-ginsburg-interview-full-transcript

Greta Christina, "5 Stupid, Sexist Things Expected of Men," *Salon*, October 14, 2014, www.salon.com/2014/10/14/5_stupid_sexist_things_expected_of_men_partner/.

Michael Gryboski, "Would the Equal Rights Amendment Threaten Religious Liberty?" *Christian Post*, January 27, 2019. www.christianpost.com/news/equal-rights-amendment-threaten-religious-liberty.html

Meg Kelly, "President Trump and Accusations of Sexual Misconduct: The Complete List," *Washington Post*, November 22, 2018. www.washingtonpost.com/news/fact-checker/wp/2017/11/22/president-trump-and-accusations-of-sexual-misconduct-the-complete-list/?noredirect=on&utm_term=.fbef571fcc2d

United Nations Development Fund for Women, "Progress of the World's Women," 2000–2015. www.unwomen.org/-/media/headquarters/media/publications/unifem/155_chap3.pdf?la=en&vs=1003

Jessica Valenti, *Full Frontal Feminism: A Young Woman's Guide to Why Feminism Matters* (Seal Press, 2007).

Gillian White, "The Invisible Work That Women Do Around the World," *Atlantic*, December 14, 2015. www.theatlantic.com/business/archive/2015/12/the-invisible-work-that-women-do-around-the-world/420372/

World Health Organization, "Violence Against Women," November 29, 2017. www.who.int/news-room/fact-sheets/detail/violence-against-women

8

LGBTQ EQUALITY

* * *

The United States' relatively poor record on LGBTQ rights isn't made better by the fact that many other nations share a similar record and dozens of nations have worse records. We started off atrociously; at the birth of our nation, in some states, sodomy was punishable by death. Thomas Jefferson, in his comparative moderation, albeit not significantly so, revised Virginia statutes so sodomy was punishable by mutilation instead of death.

Over the next two hundred years, while some notable gay and lesbian individuals managed to rise to prominence, legislation continued to target LGBTQ individuals. Consider, for example, a 1917 immigration law that banned "persons with abnormal sexual instincts," and a 1927 law adopted by New York State (in response to a play featuring a lesbian relationship) that made the performance of any play depicting "sex perversion" a misdemeanor. Such punitive and discriminatory measures intensified in the 1940s, as the U.S. military developed guidelines to exclude gay men from service and the State Department fired hundreds of people they suspected of being gay. In 1953 President Dwight D. Eisenhower issued an executive order that banned gay people from employment in the federal government; many state and local governments followed suit.

While Illinois decriminalized consensual homosexual contact in 1962, the first U.S. state to do so, it wasn't until after the Stonewall uprising in 1969 and the formation of the gay liberation movement that greater progress began to be made against antigay laws and systems: in 1975 the U.S. Civil Service Commission stopped excluding gay people from government employment; in 1982 Wisconsin passed the first lesbian and gay civil rights legislation, and in 1993 Minnesota passed the first legislation banning discrimination against transgender people. But despite this progress, backslides were common. In 1996, for example, President Bill Clinton signed the Defense of Marriage Act, which denied benefits to same-sex couples and prevented same-sex unions recognized in one state as being valid in others. In 2000, Vermont became the first state to recognize same-sex civil unions. In 2003 the U.S. Supreme Court ruled in *Lawrence v. Texas* that sodomy laws are unconstitutional, and the following year Massachusetts became the first state to legalize same-sex marriage.

Over the decades I've spent working in progressive politics, I've seen more progress for the rights and status of gay and lesbian couples than perhaps any other group. When I told my daughters about how, when I was young, there was a serious effort to legalize firing California teachers just because they were gay, it seemed hard for them to grasp, given how little one's sexual orientation seems to factor into success in the world they experience today. I recall from memory how polls posted in the *Washington Post* on support for legalizing same-sex marriages went from less than a third of the country in the 1990s to more than two-thirds of the country in 2017—steadily gaining more and more support year after year. Such a dramatic shift in public opinion over only a couple of decades is exceedingly rare, but along with such rapid change comes some unique challenges.

The battle for marriage equality was long and difficult, beginning in earnest in the 1970s when the Supreme Court declined to intervene in *Baker v. Nelson*, letting stand—for a time—the injustice that a law defining marriage as only between opposite-sex couples was constitutional. The very struggle for marriage equality enabled the growth of support groups, organizations, coalitions, and networks, all of which informed the general public and moved both public opinion and the positions of power brokers, making widespread change possible. These are essential elements for any wide-scope change efforts.

When state-level courts started revisiting this question in Hawaii and Massachusetts, the spotlight on the issue helped educate many, including state legislators that voted for fairness.

It was in the midst of this shifting landscape that the movie *Milk* was released in 2008; it told the story of Harvey Milk, the first openly gay politician to be elected to office in California in 1977. It was eye-opening in many ways, but perhaps most poignant is the movie's portrayal of the power of coming out. As Milk famously said,

> Every gay person must come out. As difficult as it is, you must tell your immediate family. You must tell your relatives. You must tell your friends if indeed they are your friends. You must tell the people you work with. You must tell the people in the stores you shop in. Once they realize that we are indeed their children, that we are indeed everywhere, every myth, every lie, every innuendo will be destroyed once and all. And once you do, you will feel so much better.

Though coming out publicly about one's sexuality means risking friendships, family, and even one's life, it also opens the door to the possibility of positive outcomes. Friends and family, even strangers, might surprise you and accept you with open arms. Even if it might take them time to accept and celebrate your identity, your coming out may trigger a growth process in them and cause them to be less close-minded going forward. And critically, from a public policy perspective, your coming out plants seeds of change. As millions of such seeds are planted, public opinion transforms, and politicians see the shifting landscape and modernize their approach to policy.

Through the efforts of individuals and organizations, growing media attention, and pubic policy initiatives, eventually the tide of change became a tidal wave that provided all the energy needed for the Supreme Court to make the right decision. Once the Supreme Court declared same-sex marriage legal in every state in *Obergefell v. Hodges* in 2015, there was such a sigh of relief among the reform-minded that many seemed to forget that there were numerous other matters still to be addressed. Of course, that progress for same-sex couples is only one aspect of what gay and lesbian folks face, and bisexual and transgender folks face a slew of additional barriers to equality and acceptance.

Representative Jared Polis (D-CO), who helped form the LGBT Equality Caucus in Congress, explained to the *Denver Post* in 2018 that, even after the Supreme Court decision, same-sex couples are often discriminated against in housing—for example, in many states they have no recourse if they are evicted from their homes. Legal protections are also needed to prevent discrimination in schools, in lending, in employment, and in many other areas; even though same-sex marriage is legal, married same-sex couples can be legally discriminated against in most states across the nation. The clean-up operation to correct remaining discriminatory laws following the tidal wave has become a long and multifaceted struggle.

Even as wins are achieved, right-wing politicos drag us backward. The Trump Administration, for example, didn't count the number of LGBTQ Americans in the 2020 U.S. Census, a critical concern since statistical evidence is key in establishing funding to counter violence and discrimination. This should not be surprising given the influence the Religious Right had within Trump's administration. As reported in a *New Yorker* article, Trump told a legal scholar not to ask his vice president, Mike Pence, about gay rights, joking, "Don't ask that guy [Pence]—he wants to hang them all!'" Trump's first attorney general, Jeff Sessions, twice supported the Federal Marriage Amendment, which would have prevented same-sex marriage. Further, according to an article in the *Atlantic*, Sessions stated that the Supreme Court case overturning laws against sodomy "divorced morality from law." With no openly LGBTQ appointments higher than ambassador as of April 2017, the Trump Administration was a who's who of anti-LGBTQ politicos, including Secretary of State Mike Pompeo, Secretary of Education Betsy DeVos, Secretary of Housing and Urban Development Ben Carson, Assistant Secretary of Health and Human Services for Public Affairs Charmaine Yoest, and many more.

Unfortunately, LGBTQ rights have become the battleground in the culture war between those clinging to discriminatory religious beliefs and a growing coalition of the nonreligious and their progressive religious allies.

Among all religious categories, nontheists are the most supportive of LGBTQ rights. According to the 2014 Pew Religious Landscape Survey, the three religious identities with the highest percentage of acceptance of LGBTQ rights in the United States are the unaffiliated or religious "nones," Buddhists, and Jews—none of which, per Pew, have majorities who believe in an intervening god. The least accepting of LGBTQ people are the most fundamentalist in religious belief, including Jehovah's Witnesses, Muslims, Mormons, and, in the greatest raw numbers, evangelical Christians. This doesn't mean that every nontheist is supportive of equality or that evangelicals are automatically bigoted, but it does suggest where one is likely to find friends, and where one isn't.

Christian fundamentalists (and other right-wing religious extremists) are anti-LGBTQ by default, because they accept their outdated religious prohibitions literally. Evidence of this beyond the above-mentioned Pew poll abounds—for example, in Title IX religious exemptions. Title IX of the Education Amendments Act of 1972 states: "No person in the United States shall, on the basis of sex, be excluded from participation in, be denied the benefits of, or be subjected to discrimination under any education program or activity receiving Federal financial assistance." Of the 139 campuses that Campus Pride listed in 2017 as the "absolute worst" for LGBTQ youth, seventy received Title IX religious exemptions to allow discrimination against LGBTQ people, and thirty-two more have similar requests pending. Of course, that's not enough for the Religious Right, so now they are seeking to change the rules so institutions don't even need to ask to discriminate with federal funds.

Mormons, Baptists, Muslims, Catholics, Methodists, and Orthodox Jews all have anti-LGBTQ prohibitions that frequently boil down to accepting LGBTQ people as long as they never act on their same-sex attractions—meaning, not only *do they not* accept LGBTQ people, but they also engage in harmful psychological shaming of natural desires.

As I will discuss in more detail in chapter 10, leaders among the

Religious Right sharpened their faith into a weapon to use against those whose presence is a threat to their narrow-minded beliefs. Forgetting their campaigns in the past, when they claimed that gays and lesbians wanted "special rights," they are now pointedly focused on seeking special religious rights of their own to discriminate against gays, lesbians, and anyone else whose life doesn't fit within their limited understanding of morality.

Unfortunately, the Religious Right and their conservative allies in government have already put pieces in place to guarantee the continuation of discrimination well into the future. George W. Bush was the first president in decades to break with the practice of seeking recommendations from the American Bar Association for appointments to the federal bench, instead taking advice from the right-wing Federalist Society. Trump followed suit, and together they appointed hundreds of federal judges who almost exclusively fit the bill of "religious conservative" and therefore are both anti-LGBTQ and anti-atheist. So while Lambda Legal reported in December 2017 that nearly a third of Trump's judicial appointments have records that "demonstrate hostility towards the rights of LGBT people," many of those without such a record probably share their prejudicial viewpoints.

Great chasms have grown between those who've accepted the growing circle of equality, and those who refuse to abandon their prejudices. While progressives seek to steadily advance the position of various groups in society, accepting nothing less than full equal treatment and opportunity, the regressive right seems to grow ever more extreme in their dehumanizing approach toward those they see as outsiders.

Bisexual Rights

Even though there's a B in LGBTQ, bisexuals are sometimes left out of equal rights debates. *LGBTQ Nation* covered a report issued by the San Francisco Human Rights Commission in 2011 that revealed that the most numerous LGBTQ category is bisexual, and that among that group the majority are female. Sadly, it concluded, "Bisexuals experience high rates of being ignored, discriminated against, demonized, or rendered invisible by both the heterosexual world and the lesbian and gay communities. Often, the entire sexual orientation is branded as invalid, immoral, or irrelevant."

While ignorance and false stereotyping is a key source of this prejudice, it may persist because bisexuality seems more compatible with dominant cisgender heterosexual culture, suggesting that bisexuals may not see as much discrimination. Some in the lesbian and gay community have also taken the view "bi now, gay later," as if bisexuality is simply a more palatable stepping stone to same-sex-only attraction. The result is that bisexual folks often feel prejudice from many quarters.

Bisexuals have a heightened exposure to sexual violence. According to a 2015 National Sexual Violence Resource Center report, 21 percent of heterosexual men have experienced sexual violence during their lifetimes, but those numbers go up to 40 percent for gay men, 43 percent for heterosexual women, 46 percent for lesbians, 47 percent for bisexual men, and a shocking 75 percent for bisexual women. That such an unthinkably high percentage of bisexual women have faced sexual violence is a wake-up call to those who overlook the challenges they face. Further, as researcher Francesca Gaiba notes, "Heterosexuals regard bisexuals (especially bisexual men) more negatively than they do lesbian and gay people." They also face the stereotype that they are more likely to carry sexually transmitted diseases than those who identify as gay, lesbian, or heterosexual.

What I've discovered regarding bisexuality follows the research for other groups that make up a segment of a minority community targeted for discrimination in our society. There are serious challenges faced that need addressing, from inaccurate stereotypes and overgeneralizations to dangerous predicaments where lives continue to be threatened—that is, until we can dispel myths and convince people to emphasize empathy and recognize our common humanity.

Transgender Rights

We may be on the cusp of a revolution of rights and consideration for transgender people. It's possible that the very recognition of this development is an aspect of what's driving the far right to their extremism as they seek last-ditch efforts to preserve their limited view of the world. In 2015, the Obama Administration hired the first openly transgender staff member in White House Liaison Raffi Freedman-Gurspan. That same year the Pentagon announced plans to lift a ban on military service by transgender people. Trump reversed that gain by reinstituting the ban.

A backlash to previous progress may also explain the urgent and widespread public debate around the "bathroom bill" in North Carolina, along with attempts to do something similar in many other states. This refers to the 2016 discriminatory North Carolina legislation (essentially repealed the following year), which stated that people may use only those restrooms and changing facilities that correspond to the sex identified on their birth certificates. While there had been no recorded incidents of transgender violence against cisgender people in bathrooms *anywhere*, the Religious Right's fear campaign absurdly made it sound like such violence was inevitable were something not done to address it. Though such language appealed to the ignorant, it appeared to backfire with the general public. More common now are bathroom bills designed to make bathrooms (especially single-user public restrooms) gender-neutral.

At the AHA's Humanist Legal Society inaugural event in 2018, titled "The Supreme Court After Kennedy," Shannon Minter, legal director for the National Center for Lesbian Rights, warned that the recent and upcoming changes in the federal bench and the Supreme Court were having a "chilling impact on federal litigation." Individuals and rights organizations feared that the danger in the federal courts was too great to risk bringing up new lawsuits or appealing them up the line. In this regard, the compostion of the courts do indeed matter. Thankfully, however, that's not the end of the story. We might yet be poised for transgender-rights breakthroughs due to the way that our longstanding laws aimed at countering discrimination against women were written—they tend to criminalize discrimination based specifically on the basis of sex. Just as laws prohibiting discrimination against people on the basis of sex prevent women from being discriminated against because of their status as women, so too should those laws prevent transgender folks from being discriminated against for their status as transgender and similarly protect other LGBTQ folks for their expressions of sexuality.

At the same inaugural Humanist Legal Society event, David Codell, the Humanist Legal Society's president, noted, "Sexual orientation discrimination is now more and more being accepted as a kind of sex discrimination." Indeed, what people are actually discriminating against is most often related to how folks aren't conforming to their expectations of masculinity and femininity. By following this very reasoning, he explained, gender identity discrimination is already accepted in many cases by the courts as a kind of sex discrimination applicable to Title IX, Title X, and other rights.

So even with the influx of unsympathetic judges to the federal bench that are bound to prove problematic for many areas, there's still some optimism about using the courts to advance transgender rights.

As activist and writer Sikivu Hutchinson said in a 2018 article for *Religion Dispatches*, "You can't advocate for LGBTQQ (lesbian, gay, bisexual, transgender, queer, and questioning) enfranchisement without confronting all of the mechanisms that criminalize queer and trans youth of color and make them at greater risk for being incarcerated, placed in foster care and/or becoming homeless." And according to the Human Rights Campaign the same year, "While the details of these cases differ, it is clear that fatal violence disproportionately affects transgender women of color, and that the intersections of racism, sexism, homophobia and transphobia conspire to deprive them of employment, housing, healthcare and other necessities, barriers that make them vulnerable."

This is why a commitment to addressing social justice intersectionally makes so much sense. Statistics bear out that discrimination against various groups is linked. Addressing them in a coordinated way is bound to be a benefit to nearly everyone. Arguably, even those who will be giving up the most privilege in order to level the playing field will benefit from a stronger, safer, more successful society.

Policy Priorities

A survey of 1,440 participants in LGBTQ Pride events by the National Gay and Lesbian Task Force (taken just before the Supreme Court ruled in favor of marriage equality) found that after marriage, folks' top priorities were challenging anti-LGBTQ discrimination and addressing hate violence and harassment.

One of the top federal priorities is passage of the Equality Act. Introduced by Democrats in the House of Representatives by David Cicilline (RI) and in the Senate by Jeff Merkley (OR), Tammy Baldwin (WI), and Cory Booker (NJ), the bill's 241 original cosponsors are the most of any piece of pro-LGBTQ legislation received upon introduction. This bill would have a sweeping impact, providing LGBTQ protections in employment, education, housing, and other key areas of life. It would write sexual orientation and gender identity protections into several existing laws, including the Civil Rights Act, the Fair Housing Act, and more. In preparation for a return to the majority, Rep. Nancy Pelosi (D-CA) announced that this legislation would be a top priority in 2019. The opposition followed suit, when it started the #Gone2Far campaign that grossly misrepresented the Equality Act as the "Pedophilia Act."

Of special interest to the humanist community is the Do No Harm Act, which attempts to limit the Religious Freedom Restoration Act (RFRA). RFRA was supposedly passed to help folks from minority faiths to be able to express their faith without the burden of government targeting them for discrimination, but the law was ill-conceived because jurisprudence already existed to prevent such viewpoint discrimination. For instance, in *Church of Lukumi Babalu Aye. v. City of Hialeah*, the Supreme Court found the city council's ordinances preventing animal sacrifice just after the Santeria-based church announced its establishment there to be unconstitutional because they unfairly singled out practices of the church. This is one of a number of examples where the courts disallow government intrusion into religious practices, meaning that no new laws were needed to address the same. What RFRA ended up doing was opening up the door to religion to be used as a shield to avoid laws, especially discrimination laws. The Do No Harm Act, introduced in the House of Representatives by Joe Kennedy (D-MA) and Bobby Scott (D-VA), appropriately exempts areas of law where RFRA has been used to bypass federal discrimination protections. While the AHA would favor an outright repeal of RFRA, Do No Harm is a good alternative.

Sometimes overlooked, policy development on aging LGBTQ populations is needed. As Robert Espinoza, vice president of policy at PHI, wrote in 2016, "Researchers and practitioners consistently describe LGBT elders as exhibiting smaller support networks, aging with higher rates of disability and chronic illness, and experiencing discrimination across long-term care." To address these needs, policy research and reporting began to produce significant results back in 2010 and now, with the benefit of that data, according to Espinoza, we must develop the skills and knowledge of professionals working in long-term care, widen housing options, and fund local aging resources specific to LGBTQ elders.

Policy needs for the LGBTQ community are also highlighted by what the opposition absurdly sees as an attack on nature. Writing for the far-right Family Research Council in 2018, Peter Sprigg attempted to frame anti-LGBT prejudice as science-based and starts off with a convoluted argument that being gay or lesbian isn't even an identity. This approach is intended to free social conservatives from self-doubt, so they can comfortably discriminate against LGBTQ people for their natural behavior and self-advocacy—for if it isn't an identity, then they are not denigrating people for who they are. This is so important to expose since it's how otherwise good people are lured into such hateful, regressive discrimination and right-wing activism. Sprigg then goes on to further pave the way for bigotry by arguing that people aren't "born this way," that it is partly the result of abuse, and that they have the option to choose not to act on their attractions. He even maintains that reorientation therapy to make people straight is a viable and positive path since, as he maintains, being LGBTQ is physically and mentally harmful. (Of course, this wrongheaded view contrasts with actual research that demonstrates the real harm of attempting to pass as straight.)

After trying to delegitimize transgender and nonbinary people, Sprigg finally arrives at his policy recommendations:

Neither lawmakers nor counselors, pastors, teachers, or medical professionals should participate in or reinforce the transgender movement's lies about sexuality—nor should they be required by the government to support such distortion. In recent years, public discussions about homosexual and transgender issues have taken an ominous turn—ominous, that is, for the future of democracy, academic freedom, freedom of speech, and freedom of religion.

While it isn't spelled out, the agenda here is clear: provide cover for bigots, delegitimize LGBTQ people's claim to equal treatment under the law, and raise religious freedom as a shield for those who wish to limit the rights of others.

Conservative politicians seem to be using Sprigg's work as a playbook, such as when Kansas passed a law permitting faith-based adoption agencies to turn away LGBTQ couples, even if the agencies receive government funds. Fortunately, as Kelsey Dallas reported in the *Deseret News*, newly elected Democratic Governor Laura Kelly planned to direct the relevant agencies not to enforce that particular legislation.

In truth, LGBTQ equality is good for society. As Charles Radcliffe wrote in 2016 for the World Economic Forum, "Every trans youth thrown out of home or forced to miss out on an education is a loss for society. Every gay or lesbian worker driven to leave their job or even their country is a lost opportunity to build a more productive economy." LGBTQ equality is good for our hearts. As Oscar Wilde once wrote, "Keep love in your heart. A life without it is like a sunless garden when the flowers are dead." And working for LGBTQ equality is good for the progress of all rights.

If we are allies in the struggle for LGBTQ equality, or for the rights of any minority group facing prejudice of which we are not a member, we should follow more than lead. Those who are the target of discrimination will be more likely to see all the angles and better understand their own needs and aims than we ever could. That may seem obvious, but often well-meaning allies overlook this point. Unless invited to play a specific leadership role by members of the minority group, allies can still provide needed leadership in their own communities by educating, informing, and persuading others. Examples of this abound: white folks explaining to other white folks why All Lives Matter is a problematic slogan; male gamers intervening to stop the sexism of their fellow male gamers; white women ensuring that Black women, Latinas, and others are represented in their struggles. When it comes to LGBTQ rights, allyship is especially critical as members of each letter (as well as others not listed) face unique challenges, and our best hope is to unite to lift the prospects of everyone through a lifelong process of building relationships based on trust, consistency, and accountability with marginalized individuals and groups of people.

As author Leslie Feinberg wrote in *Transgender Liberation: A Movement Whose Time Has Come,*

> Like racism and all forms of prejudice, bigotry against transgender people is a deadly carcinogen. We are pitted against each other in order to keep us from seeing each other as allies. Genuine bonds of solidarity can be forged between people who respect each other's differences and are willing to fight their enemy together. We are the class that does the work of the world, and can revolutionize it. We can win true liberation.

Whether we are struggling for our own rights and acceptance or working as allies, however slow, however many backlashes we must address, success is achievable.

* * *

Recommended Reading

Kelsey Dallas, "A Constant State of Red Alert: How Political Polarization Affects Religious Freedom Debates," *Deseret News*, January 25, 2019. www.deseretnews.com/article/900052444/a-constant-state-of-red-alert-how-political-polarization-affects-religious-freedom-debates.html

Robert Espinoza, "Protecting and Ensuring the Well-Being of LGBT Older Adults: A Policy Roadmap," *Generations* 40, no. 2 (September2016).www.jstor.org/stable/26556215?seq=1#metadata _info_tab_contents

Eric Ethington, "New Report Highlights Discrimination Against Bisexuals by Both Gays and Straights," *LGBTQ Nation*, March 15, 2011. www.lgbtqnation.com/2011/03/new-report-highlights-dis-crimination-against-bisexuals-by-both-gays-and-straights/

Leslie Feinberg, *Transgender Liberation: A Movement Whose Time Has Come* (World View Publishers, 1992).

Francesca Gaiba, "Prejudice Against Bisexuals Is Harming Their Health," *Role Reboot*, March 2, 2017. www.rolereboot.org/sex-and-relationships/details/2017-03-prejudice-bisexuals-harming-health/index.html

Gay Straight Alliance for Safe Schools GSAFE, "A Timeline of Lesbian, Gay, Bisexual, and Transgender History in the United States," 2004. www.gsafewi.org/wp-content/uploads/US-LGBT-Timeline-UPDATED.pdf

Sikivu Hutchinson, "Atheists of Color Transcend Opposition to Religion and White Atheist Privilege in Working for Social Justice," *Religion Dispatches*, February 20, 2018. religiondispatch-es.org/atheists-of-color-transcend-opposition-to-religion-and-white-atheist-privilege-in- working-for-social-justice/

David Masci and Micheal Lipka, "Where Christian Churches, Other Religions Stand on Gay Marriage," Pew Research Center, December 21, 2015. www.pewresearch.org/fact-tank/2015/12/21/where-christian-churches-stand-on-gay-marriage/

Pew Research Center, "Religious Landscape Survey," 2014. www.pew-forum.org/religious-landscape-study/

Robert Trivers, *The Folly of Fools: The Logic of Deceit and Self-Deception in Human Life* (Basic Books, 2014).

9

ENVIRONMENTAL POLICY

* * *

What environmental policy should we pursue as humanists? How do we address not only the climate crisis but also the justice-based issues associated with it? The positions we take should flow directly from our core humanist principles.

Philosophical Foundations

Humanists, when presented with the evidence—shrinking glaciers, rising surface temperatures, and rising sea levels—typically draw the obvious conclusion that climate change is both real and accelerating. We are also likely to accept our role as humans in making it steadily worse. Knowing we are the perpetrators of species extinctions, infertile soils, undrinkable waters, and similar hardships, we should thus take responsibility for correcting our course. Not expecting any higher power to save us at the last minute, we should accept that now is the time for us to buckle-down and to make some sacrifices so generations to come will have a planet to enjoy.

Our empathy, and the compassion and egalitarianism that flow from it, also encourage us to act on environmental justice issues. In our compassion for the plight of others we can see that environmental problems disproportionately impact minorities and women. For instance, according to a 2013 Environmental Protection Agency study, 71 percent of African Americans live in counties that violate federal air pollution standards. Black Americans are three times more likely to die from asthma-related problems than white Americans. Many communities of color lack safe drinking water, swim near waste-contaminated beaches, and live near polluted flood waters. And indigent Black and Brown children are eight times more likely to be poisoned by lead. The growing climate problem means that such communities will soon have to pay more for basic necessities, with rising prices outstripping growth in wages. As humanists, we should understand that the climate crisis is not just an existential threat in the long term but also a social justice issue in the near term.

Nonhuman Life

When considering the value we place on the environment, it's worth exploring whether humanism is an anthropocentric worldview, the concept that humans are the only, or primary, holders of moral standing. Should human comfort and convenience be prioritized over all else? Is the only value nonhuman life holds entirely in relation to our own? Or is this kind of pure anthropocentrism short-sighted because it fails to take into consideration the real intrinsic value of other life?

Generally speaking, we do value human life the highest, and there's nothing wrong with that. If I had the chance to save a person working in a kennel that was burning down versus saving dozens of dogs, I'd join the vast majority in choosing to save the human. But there's a difference between that and failing to appropriately value nonhuman animals.

Humanists commonly recognize that we are part of an interconnected web of life and that anything significant that impacts one strand can shake the entire web. That's one reason why we're frequently such good environmentalists and support efforts to combat the climate crisis. Humans may be our understandable first interest, but all life and the biosphere itself have value that must be recognized every time we discuss the importance of humanity.

How do we assess the value of all nonhuman life? Some theists feel entitled to animals as a god-given right, and some animal rights activists might choose to save the dozens of dogs over the human in the thought experiment about the burning kennel. Most humanists tend to be more comfortable seeking a middle path between such endpoints. It's likely impossible to successfully quantify relative value of living things, but even thinking about it may help us recognize that each living thing does indeed have some value. How many chimpanzees would equal the value of a single human life? Five? Ten? Twenty? Even the least sensitive humanist likely wouldn't make the number limitless. If we're considering dogs perhaps we'd be looking at a higher number. Birds might be higher still. There must be a way to value all life in the biosphere that contributes to our interconnected web— from the smallest organism to the largest.

Think about the *Star Trek* perspective where there's a prime directive not to interfere with the internal development of alien civilizations and a practice of aiming to treat them with respect and value. Even when other life forms they found weren't as advanced as humans, they weren't seen solely for their utilitarian benefit to humans. We might then construct a similar understanding of nonhuman animals and other life as retaining value independent of humanity.

When we think of *Star Trek*, or the recent real-life discovery of another eight-planet star system in our galaxy, we can more easily see that things can have value beyond what we humans designate. Bill Nye reminds us of our minor role in the universe, saying, "We are just a speck, on a speck, orbiting a speck, in the corner of a speck, in the middle of specklessness." Our great universe surely contains other valued entities, some of which are likely more advanced than we are. To value something, you just need the capacity to recognize and appreciate that value. Even here on Earth we have other species (like the apes) that value their families and communities.

A number of folks I've chatted with in recent years fit the humanist definition but are wary of identifying with our philosophy by name since they worry it implies a disregard for nonhuman animals. It'd be helpful to our movement if we articulated a broader statement so such people would be more comfortable attaching themselves to our cause.

While humans may be the most intelligent life on the planet, other animals are quite intelligent as well and are sometimes better community members than we are. In some ways humans are possibly the biggest blight on the planet, killing off species, nearly eliminating life from some geographies, and accelerating climate change. But certainly that doesn't mean we should be eradicating ourselves when we know we can do better. We are smart enough and capable enough to improve the quality of life on this planet, not just for ourselves, but for other life as well. That should be a goal of ours. We can start by ethically reducing, over time, the rate of the world's population growth, and we can—and should—do our part to make things better instead of worse. Doing so will also help preserve some of the wonder of the natural world.

During my first solo camping trip when I was nineteen, I hiked alone along the Appalachian Trail in the middle of Virginia. As I reached the top of a ridge, I stepped out of a canopy of trees and entered a meadow where the sun shone clearly on wildflowers, berry bushes, and an array of life. Looking up, I saw a family of bald eagles flying silently just above me. The serenity of my surroundings, the fractal patterns around me, and the majesty of the eagles filled me with a sense of awe and wonder—and recalling it, I am reminded that peak experiences need not rely on transcending reality. I'm always thrilled at finding nearly untouched spaces and exploring the life that thrives on our planet. Unfortunately, it seems more and more that such places are hard to find.

Humanity benefited over the past century from technological innovations and societal changes that have allowed us to reduce infant mortality and live longer, healthier lives. But this is not without its consequences as the planet and governments around the world struggle to deal with a rapidly growing global population.

Rampant pollution, food shortages, and conflict over increasingly scarce resources rise unabated. Our planet's ecosystem is hardly infinite in its resources to supply us what we need to sustain life or withstand our heedless actions that continue to degrade it. In fact, according to the World Wildlife Fund, humankind is already overusing the renewable resource capacity of Earth's biosphere by 50 percent. As more of our children survive infancy (something that wasn't confidently expected less than a century ago) and develop into adults who drive vehicles, eat livestock and crops, and have large families of their own due to choice, faith, or a lack of family-planning resources, this planet will suffer. And we're finding that things like food, jobs, and education aren't guaranteed.

As climate justice and other environmental issues gain attention across the country and around the globe, it's worth remembering the words of "Humanism and Its Aspirations" (the third and most recent Humanist Manifesto), which reminds us of our "planetary duty to protect nature's integrity, diversity, and beauty in a secure, sustainable manner." The humanist commitment to the environment didn't start with that statement either—it was prominent in its predecessor document decades earlier, which read:

> In learning to apply the scientific method to nature and human life, we have opened the door to ecological damage, overpopulation, dehumanizing institutions, totalitarian repression, and nuclear and bio-chemical disaster. Faced with apocalyptic prophesies and doomsday scenarios, many flee in despair from reason and embrace irrational cults and theologies of withdrawal and retreat.

Today, humanist environmentalists David Suzuki, Sylvia Earle, and Lester R. Brown, along with allies like Al Gore and Jane Goodall, are confronting these challenges instead of fleeing from them.

This is why it's so important to support the efforts of governments and private organizations that seek to promote family planning and help people to cooperatively decide to reduce population growth and live sustainable lifestyles. Programs that educate us about—and prevent—food waste, for example, or that broadly distribute contraception, or that help combat environmental degradation, are absolutely crucial if our children are to live in a world that can sustain them. The United Nations recognized this need for action in a 2014 report on sustainability, which stated the now obvious: "We must act now to halt the alarming pace of climate change and environmental degradation, which pose unprecedented threats to humanity."

Humanists hold a strong conviction that every human being is born with inherent dignity and the right to a life free from unnecessary pain and suffering. That sense of humanitarianism, combined with humanism's emphasis on scientifically accurate information and the role of technology in improving our quality of life, leads to powerful support for family planning, living within our means, and other efforts meant to address the problems we face today.

Contraception is the key aspect of proper family planning, vital in poorer countries since families there often struggle to feed, clothe, and shelter their children. Education must play a central role in these programs to ensure their overall effectiveness. And there's a special need to remove barriers to educating young girls and women. Several studies correlate such education with a decrease in the number of unwanted pregnancies and a decrease in the poverty rate.

While some traditional religious groups refuse to participate in comprehensive family planning efforts and claim that the distribution of contraceptives is immoral or even evil, humanists see them as a means by which individuals can gain autonomy over their bodies, better plan for their future, and lead happier lives. Unlike fundamentalists and the faith-based organizations they support, humanists don't rely on a god to fix things, don't rely on an afterlife to improve our lot, and don't have archaic prohibitions about contraception, abortion, or other means of providing families with planning options. That's why population dynamics matter so much to humanists—we humans have the ability and the responsibility to protect our planet.

Thankfully, some traditionally religious folks also appreciate the need to act as good stewards of what they see as creation. It's a good thing they feel this way, or we wouldn't have the critical mass to effect necessary change. The AHA's 1990 Humanist of the Year, E. O. Wilson, was on the right track when he wrote *The Creation: An Appeal to Save the Earth*, which calls for scientists, religious leaders, and other individuals to set aside their differences to save the environment. Only together can we address the challenges before us and support a framework that will allow generations to come to live and thrive.

At the end of the day, these population dynamics and their consequences impact everyone. But humanists are natural leaders in the effort because we understand that this is the only life we have, and this planet is the only place we have to live it.

Standard of Living, or the Environment?

There are many challenges and trade-offs to consider when we seek to address environmental degradation. Perhaps today's greatest challenge is grappling with how to raise worldwide standards of living in an equitable manner while simultaneously addressing the continuously deteriorating environment, upon which our very existence depends.

Think about the great lifesaving work the Bill and Melinda Gates Foundation is doing to reduce malaria deaths and UNICEF's work to support child health and nutrition. Of course we support these good works, but they will result in more people surviving and increasing their standards of living, which will likely have a negative impact on the environment. This leads to tough moral questions about what we prioritize in our efforts to both help struggling populations and safeguard the environment.

Fortunately, there are some areas we can expend our energies that will help with both aspects. Education about environmental degradation, family planning, and conservation can go a long way toward improving global prospects for the future while helping individuals in their specific situations.

As with other serious questions in humanism, we have to learn from history when we address the present. AHA's 2016 Humanist of the Year, Jared Diamond, details some success stories that actually worked in his books *Collapse* and *Guns, Germs, and Steel*. In past Japanese and New Guinean societies, for example, people learned to avoid the devastating environmental effects of deforestation by replanting trees at rates that exceeded harvesting of their natural resources. In more recent years, Costa Rica leveraged ecotourism to its benefit, and Denmark now generates most of its energy from renewable sources.

The island of Hispaniola provides a strong example as well, with its two countries, the Dominican Republic, to the east, and Haiti, to the west. While their differing colonial histories were certainly a factor in what we see today, environmentalism also played a major role. Whereas, as Diamond explained, Haiti didn't address deforestation, the Dominican Republic actually made illegal logging a crime against state security. This policy ultimately led to the killing of loggers in military raids. While most of us would be appalled to even consider such an extreme militaristic response to the problem, this policy indicates just how serious the government was about conservation. The different orientation toward forest conservation by the Dominican Republic versus Haiti contributed to a radically different reality between the Dominicans and their Haitian neighbors. In Haiti, clear-cutting led to massive soil erosion, reduction of land for crops, and widespread food shortages. While the Dominican Republic is far from rich, its economy is much more robust than the economy of Haiti, the single poorest country in the Western Hemisphere.

Diamond also pointed out some spectacular failures we can learn from, such as when Easter Island was deforested to the point the island could no longer sustain its once-robust culture. He even pointed out how it was a logical personal economic decision, but a devastating decision for their society, to cut down the last tree on the island. We have to be forward thinking and implement the necessary regulations and norms in our culture so it doesn't become advantageous to damage our resources beyond recovery.

While there are declines evident around the world in places where deforestation has gone unchecked, we can gain encouragement from the successes and be optimistic that if we make the effort, social transformation can and will happen. That said, we should have a complete picture of what we're up against and how far-reaching environmental issues can be.

For example, Diamond offers an explanation for the horrific ethnic cleansing in Rwanda that's completely separate from the ethnic hatred between Hutus and Tutsis. Instead of tragically preventable ethnic violence, Diamond paints a picture of unsustainability that was headed toward an inevitable train wreck. He describes how *years* before the human disaster, Rwanda experienced a few years of unusually high rainfall, which resulted in significantly increased crop yield and a major baby boom. On top of that environmental coincidence are Rwanda's inheritance practices, where sons split the land of their fathers. That led to steadily diminishing land for food that accelerated dramatically during this time of population increase. The ratio of persons per acre had been gradually increasing for years, but spiked—significantly beyond the capacity of the land to support the people—just before the disaster, when 40 percent of the people were consuming at or below famine levels.

In the analysis of the resultant massacre, it was discovered that just as many Hutus were killed by Hutus as were killed by Tutsis, and Tutsis were killing Tutsis as well. The evidence shows this was no accident. Diamond's explanation connects the facts: he argues that ethnic rivalry was the spark that ignited the fuel of overpopulation and impending starvation into a battle for resources.

Unfortunately, this situation is going to be more common worldwide as global population continues to explode. As Al Gore mentions in *An Inconvenient Truth*, we've already surpassed the number of people our planet can handle for a sustained period. We may not be too many decades from a time when crises like the one in Rwanda are seen around the globe.

I don't have all the answers but am convinced that we need to act quickly on broad-scope measures that will address the strains of overpopulation on our planet and reverse our negative global trajectory. Behavioral changes are needed that reduce our ecological footprint. Global lifestyle changes are needed so that we lessen the burden we place on our planet and can live better lives. While there's no silver bullet answer to the ecological conundrums we now face, waiting for disaster is just not a humanist option. Let's use all we know to alleviate the problems now, and use humanist reasoning to find better solutions for the future.

Humanists help ourselves by being active in environmental as well as other social justice measures. Being a humanist should suggest that we recognize the responsibility to maintain the earth as an interesting and wonderful place to live—its plants, animals, lakes, and skies need to be maintained, not turned into junk piles, toxic dumps, and deforested wastelands.

We need to include kindness to nonhuman animals because cruelty or indifference to the suffering of other animals is not a sign of a joyful life being lived well. We need to check our population growth because we don't need more and more individuals who must struggle daily just to survive. We need to make the world a better place for ourselves, for future generations, and for all of life as we know it. These things are the core of humanism.

Environmental Policy Progress

While some individuals engaged in environmental activism in the early decades of the United States, robust measures first came in to consideration with the establishment of the U.S. Department of Interior in 1849. Among its varied responsibilities, the Department of Interior manages the public parklands and is the nation's main conservation agency. In 1872, Yellowstone became the world's first national park. In the first decade of the twentieth century, President Theodore Roosevelt (who once resided in the same building that is now AHA's national headquarters) demonstrated that he was the "conservation president" by bringing millions of acres of land into the U.S. Forest Service, including fifty wildlife refuges and 150 national forests. (Unfortunately, that was made possible by stealing land, dislocating indigenous people, and allowing those who stayed only the opportunity to promote tourism with tokenism and marginalization.) Later, Congress created the National Park Service in 1916 to better manage the increasing size of the park system.

Since those early efforts there have been a handful of key governmental actions that have had a significant impact. First among them was the Clean Air Act, signed by President Lyndon Johnson in December 1963, which was the initial effort to control national air quality and one of the most comprehensive in the world. Amendments in 1970, 1977, and 1990 gave the Environmental Protection Agency (EPA) power to set increasing air quality standards and address concerns like acid rain and ozone depletion.

In 1966, the Endangered Species Preservation Act was made law in order to protect endangered and threatened species and allows government to take land into federal custody as needed in order to protect certain fish and wildlife. It also bans killing endangered species within national wildlife refuges. It was extended with the Marine Mammal Protection Act, and the language for both acts expanded over time to disallow the harassment, capture, or killing of mammals without permit.

In December 1970, President Richard Nixon formed the EPA to enforce laws that protect the environment and public health. Importantly, this was likely spurred by the twenty million people who demonstrated and attended teach-ins on environmental topics on April 22 of that year in what was the first Earth Day celebration in the United States. The EPA performs many critical safety and conservation efforts. In its first two decades of operation, the EPA's Energy Star program has saved sixteen billion dollars on energy bills, along with the resources that would have been needed to fuel that energy. The EPA also regulates and monitors fuel economy, develops radiation protection guidelines and standards, and helps organize oil-spill prevention and preparedness, among other priorities.

The Clean Water Act, signed by President Nixon in 1972, addresses water quality standards and governs pollution of the nation's waterways. Administered by the EPA, it ensures that wetlands are preserved and protects any "relatively permanent, standing, or continuously flowing bodies of water forming geographic features."

The Montreal Protocol on Substances that Deplete the Ozone Layer was a critical action taken in 1987 that addressed the production of chlorofluorocarbons that deplete atmospheric protections. The Institute for Governance and Sustainable Development indicates that well over a million cases of cancer have been prevented by this treaty.

Environmental Justice Today

Making a difference starts with each of us. According to a 2017 study by climate scientists Seth Wynes and Kimberly A. Nicholas, the most effective thing folks can do to reduce greenhouse emissions and climate impact, by far, is to have one less child—it's more than twice as effective as all other studied activities combined and reduces annual CO_2 by nearly sixty tons per year. After that, they recommend living car-free, avoiding airplane travel, and buying green energy as the next most effective steps. Smaller but still useful decisions we can make include: eating a plant-based diet, washing clothes in only cold water and hanging them to dry, recycling, and upgrading to LED lighting. Logically, congressional resolutions encouraging such behavior and giving incentives to comply could be ways policy can help us make good choices. We can support organizations advocating for such changes financially and otherwise.

Next, businesses and local governments can make changes that will reduce waste and promote renewable energy. When businesses like the AHA switch to LEDs and purchase green energy and recycle, they can have a bigger impact than individuals because of the volume involved. When I was just out of college, I worked on an assembly line in a candy factory where my job was to remove Christmas wrapping from boxes of candy so that they could be rewrapped in Easter wrapping. At the end of each day, multiple truckloads of plastic wrapping paper and metallic twine would be hauled to a nearby dump. Sounds wasteful, right? This exemplifies the significant negative impact companies have when they don't follow green practices.

Local governments often can plan for residential development that is sensitive to water resources and wildlife sustainability, such as Virginia Beach's Environmental Stewardship Framework or Santa Fe's Sustainable Growth Management Plan. Local government can require impact mitigation as well, which can take the form of hazard mapping, emissions limits, and waste treatment rules. Since local governments also have a big part to play in how individuals and local businesses recycle, advocacy to those officials is time well spent.

State officials also can influence people and businesses, and in many cases can charge major polluters for the harm they cause. They can invest in clean energy, assist communities that are disproportionately impacted by climate change, and support training and other transition assistance to workers aiming to leave the fossil-fuel economy. States also handle topics like chemical-spill prevention and food-packaging regulations that can move us toward toxic-free recycled and recyclable materials. According to reporter Brad Plumer writing for the *New York Times*, progress has already been made on a number of fronts at the state level, with more wind and solar power in Maine and New Mexico, automobile pollution reduction in Maryland and Massachusetts, carbon pricing in Oregon and New Jersey, and renewable energy experiments in Hawaii and California.

Federally, all the issues mentioned thus far are possibilities for action, as is far-reaching legislation that combats the climate crisis. Energy efficiency standards, clean energy promotion, waste management, water safety, and conservation measures are among top concerns. As the 113th Congress got underway, U.S. Representative Alexandria Ocasio-Cortez (D-NY) and Senator Ed Markey (D-MA) proposed a Green New Deal. According to the Associated Press in 2019, "The nonbinding resolution calls for a '10-year national mobilization' on the scale of the original New Deal to shift the economy away from fossil fuels such as oil and coal and replace them with renewable energy sources such as wind and solar power." Further, U.S. Representative Eddie Bernice Johnson (D-TX) has made the climate crisis a focus of the House Science Committee, which she chairs.

While the Republicans do what they can to roll back the reach of the Environmental Protection Agency, limit the jurisdiction of the Clean Water Act, remove endangered species from protections, and free businesses to pollute, humanists must stand firm against such regressive actions and seek to push real progress at every opportunity.

This isn't an unpopular stand for humanists to take. According to Monica Anderson in a 2017 Earth Day story for the Pew Research Center, even though a modest majority of Republicans are concerned that "environmental laws and regulations cost too many jobs and hurt the economy," Democrats resoundingly disagree, and at least 70 percent of the general public has supported for decades "doing whatever it takes to protect the environment."

* * *

Recommended Reading

Monica Anderson, "For Earth Day, Here's How Americans View Environmental Issues," Pew Research Center, April 20, 2017. www.people-press.org/files/2016/03/03-31-2016-Political-topline-for-release.pdf

City of Virginia Beach, "Environmental Stewardship Framework, City of Virginia Beach Comprehensive Plan—It's Our Future: A Choice City," VBGov.com, 2016. www.vbgov.com/government/departments/planning/2016ComprehensivePlan/Documents/Section%202.2_%20Environmental%20Stewardship_Final_5.17.16.pdf

Jared Diamond, *Collapse: How Societies Choose to Fail or Succeed* (Penguin, 2004).

Jared Diamond, *Guns, Germs, and Steel: The Fates of Human Societies* (W. W. Norton, 2005).

Brad Plumer, "A 'Green New Deal' Is Far from Reality, but Climate Action Is Picking Up in the States," *New York Times*, February 8, 2019. www.nytimes.com/2019/02/08/climate/states-global-warming.html

Mark A. Ryan, "Turtles All the Way Down: Justice Scalia and the Clean Water Act," *Trends* 48, no. 2 (November–December 2016). www.americanbar.org/publications/trends/2016-2017/november-december-2016/turtles_all_the_way_down.html

Santa Fe County, "Santa Fe County Sustainable Growth Management Plan," SantaFecCountyNM.gov, 2015. www.santafecountynm.gov/media/files/BCCFinal2015SGMPAmendments10-27-15.pdf

Katie Valentine, "The Whitewashing of the Environmental Movement," *ThinkProgress*, September 23, 2013. thinkprogress.org/the-whitewashing-of-the-environmental-movement-638a48614972/

Worldwatch Institute, *State of the World 2014: Governing for Sustainability* (Island Press, 2014).

Seth Wynes and Kimberly A. Nicholas, "The Climate Mitigation Gap: Education and Government Recommendations Miss the Most Effective Individual Actions," *Environmental Research Letters* 12, no. 7 (July 12, 2017). iopscience.iop.org/article/10.1088/1748-9326/aa7541

SECTION III
HUMANISM
AND SECULAR GOVERNANCE

10

WHY SECULAR GOVERNMENT?

* * *

When I was an undergraduate at Mary Washington College in Fredericksburg, Virginia, I stumbled across the Thomas Jefferson Religious Freedom Monument, which commemorates the Virginia Statute for Religious Freedom. Reading the statute for the first time, I was struck both by how religious it sounded in its introduction, "Whereas, Almighty God hath created the mind free," and also how firm it was in its proscription against religious intermingling with government. It reads, in part, that all "shall be free to profess, and by argument to maintain, their opinions in matters of Religion, and that the same shall in no wise diminish, enlarge or affect their civil capacities." This statute formed the basis for the Establishment Clause of the First Amendment to the U.S. Constitution, which reads: "Congress shall make no law respecting an establishment of religion, or prohibiting the free exercise thereof."

Recognizing his significant faults, from deprioritizing the rights of Native Americans to supporting slavery's expansion, Jefferson was brilliant in his formulations about the separation of religion and government and continued to clarify his views on the subject over time. His carefully prepared and vetted letter to the Danbury Baptist Association answered their question about why he would not declare national days of fasting and thanksgiving. Its language strongly suggests that he would have objected to mottos like "In God We Trust" and to observances like the National Day of Prayer. Religious freedom, properly understood, protects us from government intrusion into religious questions and allows for expression within limits.

We seek to uphold Thomas Jefferson's "wall of separation" between church and state and to keep government secular. Upholding the wall in a fair and just manner isn't always as straightforward as it sounds, however. Like other freedoms, religious freedom is supposed to end where another's freedom from intrusion begins, but in recent years religious freedom has become a duplicitous cover for religious bigotry, and a wedge for the insertion of a plethora of special rights for the religious that discriminate against all who don't believe as the majority does.

Religious Bigotry

The idea of religious freedom was conceived as a shield protecting against government overreach when it comes to religious matters. All Americans, be they Christian, Jewish, Muslim, atheist, and so on, should have the freedom to practice their faith or worldview free from burdensome government regulation or required participation; faith and other individual thoughts are private waters that government should not wade into except in extreme circumstances.

Jefferson's Virginia Statute for Religious Freedom communicates this perspective well, interestingly enough, emphasizing our freedom from government imposition of faith, an aspect of religious freedom too often overlooked today. The statute states (admittedly in outdated gendered terms) that

> no man shall be compelled to frequent or support any religious worship, place, or ministry whatsoever, nor shall be enforced, restrained, molested, or burthened in his body or goods, nor shall otherwise suffer on account of his religious opinions or belief; but that all men shall be free to profess, and by argument to maintain, their opinion in matters of religion, and that the same shall in no wise diminish, enlarge, or affect their civil capacities.

Unfortunately, the shield of religious freedom has often been transformed into a sword by religious conservatives who seek to force their faith on others and use that faith as an excuse to discriminate against their fellow Americans free from legal repercussions. Take, for instance, the passage of various state Religious Freedom Restoration Acts, which tend to go even further than the federal version of this law and specifically protect private citizens from civil penalties for discriminating against others because of religiously motivated views. Religious freedom should mandate government religious neutrality, but statements by a number of public officials seem to reject this idea, particularly at the expense of the nonreligious. Speaking at a high school in 2016, Supreme Court Justice Antonin Scalia went as far as to say religious neutrality just doesn't exist, specifically asserting so with his question, "there is no place for that in our constitutional tradition . . . to be sure, you can't favor one denomination over another but can't you favor religion over nonreligion?"

That's why the right-wing legal group, Alliance Defending Freedom, joined churches challenging a Massachusetts law that prohibits gender-identity discrimination in public accommodations like restaurants and meetings open to the public. Religious services are already exempted from the law, but some remain upset that they can't discriminate when they rent their space for other events open to the public. At the moment, social conservatives are using everything at their disposal to find ways to halt the progress of LGBTQ rights. They are supporting cake shops, caterers, and wedding planners who don't want to provide services to same-sex couples. They are supporting doctors, nurses, and other medical professionals who want to avoid helping LGBTQ patients. And they are supporting politicians and government workers who similarly want to use their faith as a reason to deny services and support. As discussed in chapter 8, the Religious Right would have us believe that they aren't discriminating against people, only their sexual behavior and declared identity, as if that distinction were one that reduces their bigotry.

This transformation of religious freedom, from a defensive barrier between people and the government, into a weapon used to discriminate, not only fans the flames of prejudice but also weakens the overall health of religious freedom in our country. This is because majority beliefs are seen as a civic virtue when they receive government support. This creates a preferred religion and belief that automatically relegates others to second-class status. The U.S. government's relentless support of religion over nonreligion is one reason prejudice against nonbelievers remains as strong as it does in the United States, as opposed to other democratic countries such as Norway, where secular thinking is more highly valued. In such an environment those identifying with minority faiths and philosophies are alienated and may even fear government reprisal for how they think and believe. That's not religious freedom.

Special Rights for the Religious

As progressives, we're most often inclined to side with minorities when government and business act in a way that prevents their free expression. This is true, for example, when we hear about Sikhs exercising their right to wear turbans (the *dastaar*), when Jewish students choose to pray silently before a test, or when Muslims seek authorization to build a mosque. Those are basic to religious expression as they involve chosen dress, unobtrusive thought, and the right to assemble—and they don't interfere with the rights of others. What's more, these are matters that shouldn't need special religious protection because they are exceptions to rules that shouldn't exist in the first place. We shouldn't have laws against headwear, religious or otherwise. Kids should be allowed to engage in nondisruptive thought or prayer as they see fit without any special rules spelling it out. And governments shouldn't be in the business of approving some religious buildings differently from secular ones.

This may sound jarring to the ears of many progressives, but complete religious freedom isn't possible or desirable. Some religious ideas would be unthinkable to allow, such as Old Testament decrees to apply a death penalty for cursing a parent, having same-gendered or premarital sex, taking the lord's name in vain, and so on. Consistent with scripture or not, some Muslim leaders believe that leaving Islam is also punishable by death. Then there's the concept embedded in some faiths that religion and state should be merged—that logically can't work for more than one faith at a time. So everyone should agree that at least some religious practices that are inconsistent with modern law shouldn't be allowed. Instead, religious freedom should exist only as long as it doesn't interfere with the rights of others. As the aphorism goes, "Your right to swing your arm ends where my right not to have my nose struck begins."

Unfortunately, there are religious expressions currently being allowed even though they have inherent conflicts with the rights of others. For instance, when religious clergy receive a parsonage allowance, which allows them tax-free housing and other write-offs, the result is that they aren't paying their fair share, which means that all taxpayers are subsidizing their homes and vehicles. It's unfair for atheists and agnostics to pay the living expenses of faith leaders who often specifically target them as being immoral. That's a special right granted by government to the religious, and it's morally wrong.

When parents use a religious exemption to get out of vaccinating their kids, unwittingly or not, they put others at risk. In considering this, it's worth pointing out that relatively few religions (such as Christian Science) actually oppose the use of vaccines, so most parents taking the religious exemption are doing so not based on their strongly held religious beliefs, but likely on misinformation they believe to be true about vaccines. For instance, despite popular thought to the contrary, as the Centers for Disease Control and Prevention site states, "there is no link between vaccines and autism." This fact is backed by an abundance of rigorous scientific analysis, including a massive 2019 study published in the *Annals of Internal Medicine*. When parents do exempt their children from vaccines, it doesn't just risk the health of their kids, but many others as well. That's because they are reducing "community immunity." Community immunity refers to the public resistance to a disease, whereby the majority of those who come into contact with the disease are immune, thus stopping its spread. Considering how this process works, the more who are vaccinated, the greater the community immunity effect, and the greater the chance for eliminating a specific disease entirely. But when many opt out of immunization for reasons of religion, those who are too young to have been inoculated yet or who have a serious medical reason for not being inoculated, risk being exposed to a disease they are defenseless against. That's another special right for the religious we could do without.

There's even a loophole in U.S. law that permits people engaged in religious work to be exempt from immigration laws, allowing them permanent residence, an option unavailable to their secular colleagues working for the pubic good. While the evidence suggests that long-time citizens need not worry about newcomers impacting their jobs, finances, or safety, conservative politicians so frequently stoke these fears that immigrants often face uphill battles to secure their places in our society. So it's understandable that government might help immigrants transition into becoming citizens as quickly as possible, and programs such as a special visa for those who work in charitable organizations could go a long way toward helping naturalize these folks working in the service of the larger community. But it must be available to all, and not just be another special right for the religious.

Students who choose to pray to themselves before classes, or before school-sponsored sporting events, are exercising their freedom of thought. Such private practices shouldn't be discouraged, but neither should they be encouraged by those in authority because that would inappropriately intrude on people's personal beliefs and convictions. The school itself, and its representatives in the bodies of teachers and coaches, aren't expressing their religious freedom when they invite others to participate in their faith; rather, they are wrongly imposing their religion on others. There have been multiple cases that deal with challenges to this straightforward concept, cases like those where coaches lead school football teams in prayer at public schools. It should be obvious to all that coaches shouldn't lead prayer since they represent the school and are emissaries of government, but sometimes it takes legal action, like that brought by the Appignani Humanist Legal Center, to convince schools of the rules. Public prayers during graduation ceremonies and mandatory school assemblies that feature religion or prayer are equally problematic.

The situation with special religious rights is a fairly modern one. While the Religious Right may have been seeking them for decades, they hit pay dirt in 2005 when the Supreme Court ruled in *Cutter v. Wilkinson* that the Religious Land Use and Institutionalized Persons Act (RLUIPA) allowed for more religious exceptions to secular rules. It used to be that the burden was on the individual to prove that the state was limiting their religious liberty. But with RLUIPA, the Religious Freedom Restoration Acts, and the *Cutter v. Wilkinson* ruling, the individual is assumed correct, and it's the government's burden to prove that any exception requested causes a substantial problem for the state. By flipping the burden of proof to the government, it's much easier to argue for all sorts of religious exceptions and special rights. The resultant flurry of legal and legislative efforts by the Religious Right to push for special rights for their religion included demands that ranged from the arguably reasonable, such as the right to wear special religious garb in a driver's license photo or to eat a special meal in prison, to the far more substantive and unfairly beneficial, such as getting free off-the-record counseling in the military.

Mutating the concept of religious freedom in such a way also impacts the justice system. As some people take advantage of special rights for the religious or use their religion as a way to discriminate, the concept that all laws apply to all Americans equally is jeopardized, which in turn weakens the very rule of law. After all, when time and time again we see people religiously exempt themselves from laws that the rest of us are supposed to follow, it starts to suggest that laws aren't immutable, and that we should all be able to pick and choose which ones apply to us. Such practices can set back attempts to achieve equal justice for all and prevent everyone from abiding by them once they are achieved.

Despite our liberal interest in protecting religious minorities, we shouldn't aim to achieve those protections through religious privileges, because they inherently discriminate against those who can't access them, and because they are abused by majorities who use them to find new ways to benefit themselves and discriminate against others—especially against nontheist minorities. We should instead reexamine every existing religious exemption and privilege with the move toward their complete removal. In cases where the exemption isn't causing harm, such as a number related to choices of dress, the rules and laws should be changed or removed so that everyone can dress as they see fit. In cases where there are legitimate public health and safety issues involved, the religious exemptions that endanger others should not be allowed.

The idea and character of religious freedom has changed over the years, and unfortunately the change has not always been for the better. But when celebrations like Religious Freedom Day are held in an inclusive (not intrusive) manner, they can remind us of the full benefit of religious freedom. Such occasions are opportunities to compare the intention of the concept with its current incarnation. And through this greater understanding we can work to restore our strong democratic tradition of a fairer religious freedom that protects us all.

The good news is that enlightened politicians are starting to catch on, and the U. S. Commission on Civil Rights even issued a report in 2016 discussing how to reconcile religious nondiscrimination principles with civil liberties. If nontheists and our progressive religious and secular allies can continue to raise attention to the issue, we might see a more even playing field in the future where all Americans are treated equally, regardless of particular beliefs and philosophies.

Religion in Schools

Keeping schools secular and neutral doesn't infringe on religious liberty, because parents can ensure that their child gets all the religious instruction they want by attending services at their house of worship, partaking in weekend religious education programs, or participating in religious youth outreach groups. Still, inappropriate religious favoritism in public schools has been around much longer than the recent Religious Right strategy to leverage religious freedom to get faith officially recognized. For decades we've seen efforts to promote abstinence only, which has been shown to increase rates of teen pregnancies, instead of comprehensive sex education. We've seen teachers refuse to teach evolution, either because they see it as undermining their beliefs, or because they want to avoid controversy. We've seen the intrusion of religion into public school textbooks that fail to teach what we know about history and science because they don't fit within the faith-based narrative. And we've seen school symbols, banners, and holiday expressions that favor one religion, usually Christianity, over all others.

With some public schools struggling, we see people turning to voucher systems as a solution to problems that were magnified by the very introduction of school vouchers. The first critical shortcoming of voucher programs is that they divert scarce public funds to help a small group of students (usually from wealthier families who have the luxury to explore alternatives) at the expense of other students, who continue to attend schools that now have even fewer resources with which to try and provide a quality education. The second central drawback of vouchers is that they are often used to fund religious education, and that situation results in taxpayer dollars being inappropriately filtered into indoctrinating kids into one brand of religion or another. It's just inexcusable to make atheists and others pay for religious education that tends to condemn them. On top of that, such religious schools aren't subject to the same regulations that public schools face, which is why some fall far below public schools in terms of safety and performance.

Whether in voucher programs, or in public school curriculums and textbooks, or as part of the Pledge of Allegiance, which kids are asked to recite every day, government intrusion into religion is divisive and a distraction to the real purpose of public education. The failure to teach the best of modern knowledge for religious reasons poses a serious threat to our nation's educational system and to current and future students. When schoolchildren are taught dated religious dogma instead of a credible academic program, their ability to function in the real world and compete for jobs is drastically diminished. Religious teachings should not come at the expense of things like science education, mathematics, literature, and history, which should always be taught based on our best current understanding of them.

The Blain Amendments

Known as the Blain amendments, dozens of states passed state constitutional amendments that bolster First Amendment separation of religion and government. The story of how they came to be is an interesting one. James G. Blain was a Republican member of Congress representing Maine between 1863 and 1876. Though criticized today by the far right as an anti-Catholic, Blain, whose mother was Catholic, was motivated by more noble aims. Along with then President Ulysses S. Grant, he was a staunch supporter of government neutrality on the question of religion, seeing potential problems with the intermingling of religion and government in state-funded parochial schools. He proposed an amendment to the U.S. Constitution that would bar state funds from being spent on religious activities, such as funding Catholic and other religious schools. The campaign was unsuccessful by just a few votes in the Senate.

Despite losing the fight at the federal level, thirty-eight states took Blaine's recommendation and added similar amendments to their state constitutions. As one might imagine, these laws have had a positive impact on church-state separation litigation at the state level, particularly with regard to issues like school vouchers, which could potentially be used to fund students at private religious schools.

The U.S. Secretary of Education in the Trump Administration, Betsy DeVos, made it her mission to lessen federal regulations on religious schools in hopes of ending the longstanding Blaine amendments; but since their enactment over a hundred years ago, with the exception of Louisiana, states have long been unable to convince their residents and legislators to remove them from state constitutions.

As reported by AHA Board Member Rob Boston in *Church & State*, it was back in 1973 when, at a Louisiana constitutional convention, "Lobbyists for the Roman Catholic Church succeeded in removing the Blaine amendment, and voters later ratified the new constitution. Louisiana immediately began funneling millions in state aid to parochial schools. Today, its public school system is regarded as one of the worst in the nation." Not surprisingly, there was no flurry of effort to retract Blaine amendments in other states at the time.

A 2016 effort to remove the Blain amendment in Oklahoma failed by a fair margin of 57 to 43 percent at the ballot box. In 2018, Amendment 8, a proposal that would have gutted Florida's Blaine amendment and opened the door to state funding of religious charter schools backfired when the state supreme court struck the measure from the ballot in the final days before the election. In an effort to make the measure more palatable to voters, conservatives had concealed the true nature of the measure by using language that implied it would only allow the state to control public schools. As a lawyer representing the League of Women Voters described to the *Tampa Bay Times*, "The Supreme Court has once again affirmed that a sponsor or a revision to the Constitution must be clear in explaining what it will do."

The continued strength and breadth of these Blain amendments has become increasingly important for church-state separation. As the federal courts are now filled by Trump-appointed and previously appointed far-right justices, the state courts, especially in states with Blaine amendments, offer more favorable avenues to pursue freedom of and from religion.

Johnson Amendment

The Johnson Amendment is a different kind of amendment from those modifying constitutions. This was a contemporaneous modification of a 1954 law that prevents religious and other tax-exempt organizations from endorsing candidates, lobbying, or engaging in other political activities. In case the loss of this piece of legislation sounds innocuous, it's worth noting that this is more than just prohibiting clergy from electioneering from the pulpit. As noxious as that is, it's nothing compared to the financial implications for elections. If the Johnson Amendment were fully repealed, churches would be permitted to give unlimited funds to electoral campaigns. And since contributions to churches are unreported, tax deductible, and unlimited, churches would become the ideal funnel for all electoral contributions. They would, in effect, be the new super PACs. They would also be worse than any previous campaign finance loopholes, because church finances aren't trackable. Not only would this offer up electoral offices to the highest bidder, but it would also have a distinctly conservative bent because of church involvement.

During his first presidential campaign, Donald Trump promised to repeal the Johnson Amendment, a move that garnered him support from many Religious Right leaders, like then Liberty University President Jerry Falwell, Jr., former Christian Coalition executive director Ralph Reed, and others. Trump repeatedly tried to fulfill his promise while he was in office.

Fortunately, the AHA saw this threat coming and started lobbying immediately against the Johnson Amendment's repeal. As soon as Trump was inaugurated and the new Congress was in session, the AHA sponsored briefings for members and staff in the House and the Senate that were attended with standing-room only. Then the AHA joined colleagues in both secular and religious movements to expose and prevent attempts to weaken this critical protection, including an executive order issued by Trump on the topic. This process began by revealing the true nature behind the executive order, which was meant to lay the groundwork for removal of the amendment. Multiple attempts to legislate the amendment away never gained the needed traction because of the steady opposition we were able to coalesce. Some such attempts were direct, such as the deceptively named Free Speech Fairness Act introduced in 2017 (House Resolution 172), which aimed to restore the free speech and First Amendment rights of churches and tax-exempt organizations by repealing the 1954 Johnson Amendment. Others were less direct, like the various additions to spending bills that sought to weaken the amendment. Now scores of organizations are keeping a close watch to be sure the amendment isn't repealed in the future.

Religious Symbolism

The one area where I get the most pushback from colleagues and allies is related to AHA's efforts to remove government-sponsored religious symbolism. The most common criticism we receive when challenging such intermingling is that this symbolism is harmless. But it's not harmless, not only because the existence of monuments like crosses on public lands are used to legally justify other government intrusions into religion, but also because the monuments themselves send a harmful message to religious minority and nonreligious families that they are unwelcome.

Another criticism is that challenging religious symbols could prevent us from allying with progressive people of faith. But in my actual discussions on such matters, I find that the vast majority of progressive people of faith are not themselves discouraged by our legal activism. For example, progressive religious leaders such as Cooperative Baptist Rev. C. Welton Gaddy, Disciples of Christ Rev. Ken Brooker Langston, and Ambassador-at-large for International Religious Freedom Rabbi David Saperstein not only do not object to our position regarding the inappropriateness of government displays of faith, but also join us in this view.

Today, God is on our money and part of our nation's motto, which religious conservatives try to get emblazoned on as many public buildings and monuments as possible. And when it comes to remembering our fallen veterans with memorials on public property, too often they are infused with religion in a way that is divisive since not everyone who dies for this country is of the same faith.

Monuments constructed to serve as memorials for veterans and casualties of wars aren't unobtrusive nonissues, but rather are serious matters. Veterans who stand among us, as well as those who made the ultimate sacrifice in service to our country, deserve our respect and recognition. I've spoken at the U.S. Naval Academy and Lackland Air Force Base and met with active duty soldiers from other branches of the U.S. Armed Forces who care about this issue. As long as public cross memorials stand unaltered, they continue to exclude those soldiers of other faiths, or no faith, who serve or who have served our nation. Disrespecting our patriotic service members like this is indecent, and it's time for it to change.

And nobody really believes that Christian Right legal teams are sincere in their statement that the cross is secular, as they claim in our Supreme Court case against the forty-foot cross in the middle of a public road in Bladensburg, Maryland—*American Legion v. American Humanist Association*. It's time the courts and the general public stop taking these obviously false claims that crosses are nonreligious as honest ones.

The Bladensburg cross's clear endorsement of Christianity fails to honor the thousands of non-Christian U.S. soldiers who have fought and died on both foreign and domestic soil. Many government-erected war memorials, whether in the form of an obelisk, pedestal, plaque, or statue, recognize the service of all veterans, regardless of their faith or lack thereof. In contrast, fundraising for the Bladensburg cross included a pledge to trust in God (the initial intent was to create "a likeness of the Cross of Calvary, as described in the Bible"). Further, the dedication of the cross was marked by an invocation and a benediction by Christian leaders, and religious services continue to be held at the public monument today. Even worse, discrimination was built into the monument itself; it lists forty-nine (presumably Christian) service members, but excludes the names of Jewish veterans from the same location and regiment.

In the Bladensburg cross case, the AHA's Appignani Humanist Legal Center urged the government to heed the rulings of the lower courts, Supreme Court precedent, the Constitution, and the calls of veterans and active service members to erect a memorial that honors all those who've bravely put us and our freedom before themselves.

Unfortunately, we lost the case. The Religious Right and its allies in government don't really want to honor all those who served or respect everyone in their communities. Efforts to insert Christian language and symbolism are plainly exclusionary, and fail to honor Jewish, Muslim, Hindu, Buddhist, Sikh, and nonreligious community members. And because of the government's involvement in the sectarian message that such memorials convey, they also violate the spirit of the Establishment Clause of the First Amendment, which forbids government endorsement of religion.

When we as a country refuse to acknowledge that our diversity is one of our greatest strengths, we dishonor the tens of thousands who fought and died to create a nation where religious views don't divide us—one in which we are able to unite in our desire to work hard and sacrifice for others and for our country.

* * *

Recommended Reading

Rob Boston, "The Blaine Game," *Church & State*, September 2002. www.au.org/church-state/september-2002-church-state/featured/the-blaine-game

Sara Chodosh, "Vaccines Don't Cause Autism, Another Massive Study Confirms," *Popular Science*, March 5, 2019. www.popsci.com/measles-vaccine-autism-link-research

Luis Granados, "Rules Are for Schmucks: The Amazing Special Privilege for Religious Immigrants," *Humanist*, June 4, 2015. thehumanist.com/voices/rules_are_for_schmucks/rules-are-for-schmucks-the-amazing-special-privilege-for-religious-immigrants

Jeff Guo, "Here's How to Use Religious Freedom Laws to Fend Off a Gay Discrimination Suit," *Washington Post*, April 3, 2015. www.washingtonpost.com/blogs/govbeat/wp/2015/04/03/heres-how-to-use-religious-freedom-laws-to-fend-off-a-gay-discrimination-suit/

Thomas Jefferson, "Jefferson's Letter to the Danbury Baptists," Library of Congress, January 1, 1802. www.loc.gov/loc/lcib/9806/danpost.html

Miriam Krule, "Why Is There a Religious Exemption for Vaccinations?" *Slate*, February 5, 2015. slate.com/technology/2015/02/religious-exemption-for-vaccines-christian-scientists-catholics-and-dutch-reform-church.html

U.S. Commission on Civil Rights, "Peaceful Coexistence: Reconciling Nondiscrimination Principles with Civil Liberties," 2016. www.usccr.gov/pubs/Peaceful-Coexistence-09-07-16.PDF

Virginia Museum of History and Culture, "Thomas Jefferson and the Virginia Statute for Religious Freedom," 2016. www.virginiahistory.org/collections-and-resources/virginia-history-explorer/thomas-jefferson

11

THE POLITICAL EDGES
OF HUMANISM

* * *

Humanists generally abhor the idea of a political litmus test for professed humanists, in part because it smacks of exclusion, which goes squarely against humanism's inclusionary default. To align humanism politically also suggests we're buying into a dogma of sorts in ideology, whereas humanists seek fair consideration of all ideas. So the notion that humanism might not be compatible with conservatism is to some extent illicit, and the idea that humanists should follow a particular ideological bent is a daring one. Nonetheless, a strong case can be made that humanists are not natural political conservatives.

Of course, there are probably a few conservatives who identify *wrongly* as humanists, such as Pope Benedict XVI (Joseph Ratzinger), who saw himself as a humanist, but meant it in the most generic of self-aggrandizing senses, as well as those who may not want to admit that they aren't humanists—it's such a positive sounding term that people don't like to reject it. I don't generally see this trait among AHA's dues-paying members or those making significant investments in humanism, but I frequently encounter someone in a local humanist group who insists that humanist groups and organizations must be open to their antiabortion, economically stingy, all-lives-matter perspectives. Group leaders are often reluctant to tell someone they aren't in the right place, even when that person holds views that are diametrically opposed to humanism, because they like to keep their doors open to all.

Accepting these caveats, are there real political conservatives who have found a true home in humanism? Let's explore that possibility. Looking at common usage of the terminology, political conservatives aren't merely people who subscribe to one or two conservative positions; they are those who follow conservatism as a general rule. A single conservative position—such as an anti–gun control stance— doesn't make someone a political conservative any more than believing in gun control would make an otherwise politically conservative person a liberal. *Merriam-Webster* defines liberal as "one who is open-minded or not strict in the observance of orthodox, traditional, or established forms or ways." What then are the positions that define a conservative ideology? They're consistent with the popular dictionary definition of conservative as "one who adheres to traditional methods or views."

An average conservative person (not just a so-called humanist conservative) would likely hold the following defining opinions:

- Abortion is wrong and should be outlawed in almost all circumstances in order to protect the sanctity of life.

- The United States has been a godly nation since its founding and the government should actively make sure it stays that way.

- Only opposite-sex attraction and relationships are normal, so there's no reason to grant LGBTQ folks the same rights and benefits as cisgender heterosexuals.

- What is good for business is also necessarily good for the United States and its people.

- Men and women, like other definable groups, have dissimilar aptitudes, which is probably why males are so successful in business.

- Retribution is an acceptable motive for the punishment of crime and for becoming involved in global conflict.

Though such positions sound extreme to the mild-mannered humanist, they are mainstream conservatism summed up. These statements form the basis for much of the official 2016 Republican Party platform plank called "A Rebirth of Constitutional Government," which includes subsections on "Defending Marriage Against an Activist Judiciary," "Protecting Human Life," and "Protecting Private Property." There's even a section on "Religious Liberty," with a view toward permitting conservative Christians to avoid laws that get in the way of their bigotry and other dated thinking. They also match up seamlessly with the declared positions of the American Conservative Union (ACU), the leading politically conservative organization.

Not an extreme group by conservative standards, the ACU sponsors the well-known Conservative Political Action Conference (CPAC) and has been the standard bearer for conservatism for decades, touted years back by President George W. Bush as "an invaluable partner in advancing our compassionate conservative agenda."

While the AHA has issued dozens of position statements that strongly oppose the above-outlined conservative viewpoints, no solitary position truly bars one from being a humanist. Nonetheless, someone who agrees with all the base conservative statements (atheist or not) might do well to consider a different philosophical home—because humanism simply isn't compatible with such a set of positions.

Most humanists who call themselves politically conservative wouldn't be embraced by "real" conservatives, those who would be appalled to associate with most nontheists. Such humanists may want to rethink their self-characterization as "conservative," since the match isn't as good as it may seem to them. For instance, I've encountered humanists who I suspect identify as conservative only because that moniker is driven by their overall rebellious personality. As nontheists they're rebelling against general society, but after being around humanists long enough they unnecessarily try to distinguish themselves from them as well. A tip-off that this is the case is when they try to qualify their conservatism by saying, "On many subjects, atheist political conservatives believe differently from their religious kindred." But such qualifications just underscore the fact that the politically conservative label doesn't fit.

Conservative viewpoints run counter to the principles outlined in "Humanism and Its Aspirations." While not all humanists are aware or closely follow this document, the point of it is that it outlines the latest consensus foundational principles of modern humanism. It fits what humanists as a whole believe and aspire toward achieving.

Atheists, by leaving behind ancient myths and discarding divine revelation as a source for knowledge, are ahead of their theistic partners when considering political questions. That said, there certainly is a sizable number of nontheistic people who refuse to part from their conservative doctrines and aren't properly labeled humanists. S. E. Cupp is a modern political commentator on CNN who isn't shy about her atheism, but she wrote a book about the left's attacks on Christianity and vigorously defends melding church and state. Men's Rights Activists, a movement that seeks to halt women's progress toward equal pay and equal work, and that misogynistically asserts their rights to women's bodies, are populated by a number of atheists, but those individuals don't display the compassion and egalitarianism common to humanists.

By definition, humanists are nontheistic and, for the purpose of self-preservation if nothing else, nontheists should support the separation of religion and government. But simply being a nontheist, rejecting the supernatural, and supporting the First Amendment doesn't make one a humanist, because humanism means more than a common reference point in nontheism. As discussed earlier, humanism's progressive outlook is undergirded by the scientific method, compassion, and egalitarianism. These principles lead humanists to be natural progressives, because each of these foundational concepts is evolutionary in nature. Science constantly updates itself as more is learned and new theories emerge based on facts that are confirmed through replicable experiments. Compassion compels us to seek better opportunities for those we see suffering around us. And our sense of egalitarianism doesn't allow us to rest comfortably with unjust inequality. Why would humanists want to conserve old ways of thinking and behaving when we can learn better ways to do both? Humanists reject outdated conventions of every form.

A combination of the rational analysis that rigorously challenges bogus claims of group superiority, together with the compassionate openness to empathize with other humans, make up the humanist assumption of equality from which many progressive positions flow. Unlike mainstream conservatives, humanists recognize the ethical responsibility of individuals and groups to treat each other equally with respect to social, political, and economic rights and privileges.

It isn't difficult to see how political positions emanate from humanism's core principles. For instance, the humanist orientation toward reason immediately discounts many arguments against equal treatment, since those are either based in flawed studies, or originate in religious belief. By connecting the dots between humanism and politics, it becomes obvious that the core principles of humanism support liberalism. So it isn't surprising that based on membership surveys, over 90 percent of humanists support reproductive rights, assisted suicide, and uncensored freedom of speech—an extraordinary level of agreement. Despite mainline churches' authoritarian structure and rigidly defined positions, most simply don't see that kind of favorable unanimity toward these issues.

Political conclusions aside, humanists must continue to explore diverse views. Not only is this liberal open-mindedness characteristic of humanism, it is also necessary for any group that so relies on disagreement and discourse to further its philosophy. Furthermore, there is plenty of room for disagreement on methods for achieving progressive goals. Some think that for humanists to address political positions at all will narrow the movement's potential for growth. Technically it does of course, since not everyone will subscribe to our progressive aims, but the many millions who do make the limitation essentially meaningless compared to our current numbers—well under a million. The steady growth of humanism and feedback from members and supporters overwhelmingly indicate that committed humanists are pleased with efforts to speak out on issues of concern. If humanists refuse to address difficult subjects, the resulting blandness will diminish the movement's potential—both in terms of numbers and effectiveness.

The Libertarian Humanist

Anyone willing to be public about their nontheism in today's environment is often a little drawn toward contrarianism and proud to see things a bit differently from the norm. So it shouldn't be too surprising to find a fair number of libertarians among nontheists, since libertarianism is also a contrarian or square-peg-in-a-round-hole type of outlook. I've come to know a number of humanists who either identify as libertarians or lean libertarian in their thinking. They reveal this with the mantra of explaining they are "socially liberal, but fiscally conservative." Those who go as far as to identify as libertarian characterize just a minority of humanists—only 2 percent in a survey of AHA members, though this percentage is likely higher within other humanist and atheist organizations that aren't so closely aligned with the left.

I've found these folks might be categorized in one of three ways, none of which is particularly favorable, so I hope those I know who feel this way will engage me in friendly debate rather than see this section as an attack on them. Personally, my thinking on this has shifted over the years and will likely continue to shift, but right now I feel that those who identify as libertarian humanists are either torturing the definitions of one or the other word, clinging to unproven theories, or are living with serious contradictions. In many cases that doesn't make them "not humanists," but it does suggest that their humanistic aims could benefit from further reflection.

First, there are a sizable number of long-time libertarians who've drifted away from a strict commitment to reduce the power of government and thus now acknowledge the need for humanism in policy. Perhaps they still lean libertarian on occasional issues, but they likely support government funding of Planned Parenthood, seek support for public schools, and aren't otherwise opposed to regulations on corporations that protect people and the environment. So, this first category of libertarian humanists aren't actually libertarian objectivists and would almost certainly have strong objections to true libertarians like David Koch, who was one of the strongest supporters of conservative causes in recent years.

Those in the second category of libertarian humanists are without exception people in a financially strong position. They might not be wealthy by some particular metric or even by their own standards, but they have no issue meeting their basic needs and are not concerned that one day they might have difficulty subsisting. These libertarians have self-interest as their primary interest. This doesn't necessarily make them bad people, because they can still have other interests, but when it comes to the bottom line, they make sure their personal policies don't negatively affect themselves. Many were raised without wealth, had to struggle to get ahead, and feel a sense of achievement for their accomplishments that bolsters their idea that others could follow a similar path if they worked in a similar way. They might have become more fiscally conservative as they became more financially secure and thus less desiring or dependent on government support in all its forms.

So many libertarians fit this mold that it skews the numbers for them overall. It's why libertarians are disproportionately wealthy and support policies that keep them that way. They might not see this themselves, but remember the popular Wikipedia definition of rationalization:

> In psychology and logic, rationalization or rationalisation (also known as making excuses) is a defense mechanism in which controversial behaviors or feelings are justified and explained in a seemingly rational or logical manner to avoid the true explanation, and are made consciously tolerable—or even admirable and superior—by plausible means.

In the third category are libertarian humanists who often are the most consistent in much of their thinking, but who have a soft spot in their heart for unproven libertarian theory. These humanists see benevolent individualism and the free market as the best means for creating more wealth and power to benefit all. While humanists are natural optimists, seeking to better the world and bolster themselves with evidence of progress and potential, these particular libertarian humanists take it a step further. They are betting that without the intrusion of government, things will be better. Most seem to distrust government, but have a strong faith in the invisible hand of the market, believing, despite evidence to the contrary, that businesses will see it in their best interest to do things for the common good.

Among the many barriers to a market-based approach to societal health is the fact that corporations are structured for the sole benefit of their shareholders. In fact, a portion of the law-governing corporations dictates that corporations must always act only in the interest of their shareholders or open themselves up to legal action from those shareholders. Precedent confirmed this as recently as the 2010 *eBay v. Newmark* case, and the Delaware Supreme Court Chief Justice confirmed this in 2015, saying, "Directors must make stockholder welfare their sole end." If shareholder interest in seeing stock prices rise conflict with an interest in public safety, public safety loses. There are folks who argue that this is a good state of affairs, such as UCLA Professor Stephen Bainbridge, who claimed in a 2015 article for the *New York Times* that without such an arrangement, "director discretion—when purportedly directed toward social responsibility concerns—could just be used to camouflage self-interest." But ultimately, when this corporation-first policy is practiced in the real world, everyday citizens lose too often.

Libertarians have explained to me that in such cases where corporations fail to act in the public good, a public scandal ensues and the shareholders ultimately lose, thus the corporation is pressed to do what's right because a corporation engaging in unsafe practices is bad for business. That may be so when unsupportive behavior is quickly revealed, but how long, if ever, will it take to discover all bad practices, across all corporations?

We don't have to look hard to see numerous examples where public interest was compromised for years, negatively affecting the lives of many people before problems were uncovered. Think of the true story of Erin Brockovich, made into a popular Julia Roberts movie, where her legal team ekes out a narrow victory against the power company PG&E for its role in poisoning scores or more people in a rural town. Despite the victory, PG&E is still posting eleven-figure annual revenue. Consider also the popular satirical comedy *Thank You for Smoking* and the more hard-hitting follow-up documentary

Merchants of Doubt, which revealed the role of the tobacco industry in keeping its products' cancerous properties from becoming public for many years. Myron Levin, founder and editor of *Fair Warning*, wrote a 2019 investigative story for the *American Prospect* that uncovered a law firm, Bracewell LLP, which specializes in helping manufacturers that take calculated risks on costly safety measures to be free from liability. Levin wrote, "Bracewell and its clients in recent years have sidelined regulations aimed at keeping toddlers from being strangled by window blind cords; avoiding carbon monoxide poisoning deaths from portable generators; and preventing thousands of finger amputations by table saws." Even when companies lose, the losses may make those caught look bad and cost them modest amounts of money, but they rarely cripple their ability to go on engaging in negative practices. And who knows how many are never caught?

One humanist I met, Charles Lee Lescher, wrote intriguing science fiction books that imagined a libertarian future threatened by a return to authoritarian governments, but as enjoyable as such fiction is to read, it doesn't reveal a plausible path to a better future for all that is founded on libertarianism. What, then, is the best approach to "conservative"-identifying humanists?

Conservative-identifying humanists are anomalies, and that's the statistical reality confirmed by any survey on religion and politics that I've ever come across. According to the 2014 Pew Religious Landscape Survey, for example, liberals are much more likely than conservatives to not believe in god, and the nonreligious are the most likely of all religious categories to be liberal on almost every issue—and that's before overlaying the humanist lens on nontheism.

Contrary voices, as long as they aren't disruptive or disrespectful, offer a positive opportunity for debate. I say positive here because debate offers an opportunity to deepen the knowledge of those debating, readies us for countering our opposition, and educates the audience who may not be as steeped in the reasons behind our humanistic conclusions. Sometimes there's an overlap between politically contrarian voices and toxic personalities, but there's no need to treat everyone with a different viewpoint as a problem. A line is only crossed when such voices shut down productive discussion, inappropriately speak for the group, or hold the group back from having a humanist impact, locally or nationally.

One change we might make is being bolder about our political interests. There is no reason humanist individuals, and local, state, and national groups, should be shy about expressing their progressive political values and acting on them by advocating for their adoption to make everyone's life better. We needn't neutralize our own effectiveness by keeping to more universal topics, and nobody benefits from concealing our agenda. If this approach alienates conservative-leaning folks to the point that they depart from humanism, they'll likely be replaced by many more who are thrilled to see a positive difference being made. Together those remaining will be better able to seek progress for humanism.

* * *

Recommended Reading

Stephen Bainbridge, "A Duty to Shareholder Value," *New York Times*, April 16, 2015. www.nytimes.com/roomfordebate/2015/04/16/what-are-corporations-obligations-to-shareholders/a-duty-to-shareholder-value

Lydia Denworth, "Conservative and Liberal Brains Might Have Some Real Differences," *Scientific American*, October 26, 2020. www.scientificamerican.com/article/conservative-and-liberal-brains-might-have-some-real-differences/

Bishop McNeill, "Wait, You're an Atheist AND a Conservative?" *Humanist*, March 10, 2014. thehumanist.com/commentary/wait-youre-an-atheist-and-a-conservative/

Republican National Committee, "Republican Platform: Ratified in 2016," 2016. gop.com/platform/

Scott Ryan, *Objectivism and the Corruption of Rationality: A Critique of Ayn Rand's Epistemology* (iUniverse, 2003).

Leo Strine. "The Dangers of Denial: The Need for a Clear-Eyed Understanding of the Power and Accountability Structure Established by the Delaware General Corporation Law," *Wake Forest Law Review* 50 (2015). papers.ssrn.com/sol3/papers.cfm?abstract_id=2576389

Michael Strupp-Levitsky, Sharareh Noorbaloochi, Andrew Shipley, and John T. Jost, "Moral 'Foundations' as the Product of Motivated Social Cognition: Empathy and Other Psychological Underpinnings of Ideological Divergence in 'Individualizing' and 'Binding' Concerns," *PLOS One*, November 10, 2020. journals.plos.org/plosone/article?id=10.1371/journal.pone.0241144

12

A SECULAR GOVERNMENT FOR ALL

* * *

On that crisp evening in February 2018, when the Congressional Freethought Caucus in the U.S. House of Representatives was born in a modest Capitol Hill townhouse, one by one four members of Congress had arrived to join Rep. Huffman, Ron Millar, and me. Each representative came without any of their staff, as if carefully aiming to maintain a low profile about attending the meeting.

Conversations began immediately and were wide ranging, from concerns about abuses in Catholic churches, to interest in prominent atheists, to what was important about the reason-based progressive approach of those gathered. The talk was peppered with humor, and drawn together by an enthusiasm that recognized the novelty of what was happening, the first gathering of freethinking members of Congress to find ways to advance causes of concern for those who don't have traditional religious beliefs.

The three delivered pizzas and the three bottles of wine from Rep. Huffman's district were nearly consumed over the course of the evening, as conversations covered a range of matters, from how to be authentic with one's constituents as an open nontheist, to whether we have faith in democracy and if that faith was being tested with Trump in office. It was quite an experience to be part of this moment in history, and to see the progress being made that I and others had spent years aiming for. During a follow-up meeting at AHA headquarters, the mission statement for the new group was hammered out, and the founding co-chairs, Reps. Huffman and Raskin, prepared the paperwork to make the caucus official.

Huffman chose to publicly announce the caucus at that year's Secular Coalition for America lobby day, for which several humanist, atheist, and freethought organizations had gathered, and had a series of positive media appearances, in which he took the opportunity to educate folks about humanism and the critical importance of church-state separation.

The response to the caucus since has been overwhelmingly positive. In fact, I received a personal congratulatory letter from UK Parliament Member Crispin Blunt and Baroness Bakewell, who are the co-chairs of Parliament's Humanist Caucus, along with Humanists UK Chief Executive Andrew Copson. That letter read, in part, "Suffice to say, the formation of the Congressional Freethought Caucus is, in our view, a serious cause for celebration. We wish you all the best of luck with the initiative, and if we can ever be of any assistance, please do not hesitate to ask." As of this writing, the caucus is up to eleven members: demographically diverse progressive Democrats who meet regularly and seek ways to make a positive impact.

This volume attempted to explore the true foundation of good public policy—philosophically, consequentially, and effectively. We looked at the benefits of public policy change itself as a path to societal progress. We looked at what it takes to be a high integrity, high-impact politician. We looked at who benefits from public policy, what the difference-making factors are in public policy, and why an intersectional approach to public policy is both natural to humanism and most effective. And, of course, we examined public policy approaches to racial justice, gender justice, LGBTQ equality, environmental policy, and secular government, taking time to recognize the nondogmatically liberal bent to humanism and how to address conservatism.

How Utopian Must Our Activism Be?

One public policy challenge not yet addressed is how to balance short-term needs with long-term aims. We know that the justice system itself needs overhauling, but do we wait for the chance to do it comprehensively, or do we take every opportunity to achieve discrete goals, such as reducing mandatory sentencing and advancing measurers that stop police brutality? Similarly, fierce debates have been waged over whether we should pass legislation protecting gays and lesbians from employment discrimination now or whether we should wait to build the support needed to pass more inclusive legislation that protects the rights of bisexual and transgender individuals as well. Seeking equal protection for nontheists, we know that prayers before government meetings are always problematic, but should we seek solely to abolish the practice, or should we seek the opportunity for nontheists to participate in invocations as an interim step?

While there are some particular bills in Congress that settle for compromise too soon, in general I feel that we can work simultaneously for short- and long-term aims. Finding the right balance can be difficult because sometimes those most in need of protection via advances in public policy are themselves involved in polarizing debates that inhibit advancement through compromise. This means that some strategies for action now can, in the name of expediency, result in choices that leave behind those most in need. But I'd argue that every positive advance moves the needle of public perception in the right direction, setting the stage for further advances. To give a practical example, let's look at our national motto, "In God We Trust."

"In God We Trust" was added in 1956 as the official U.S. national motto, pushing aside the unofficial one, *E Pluribus Unum*. It was no coincidence that this happened during the McCarthy era, which was defined, in large part, by the United States seeking ways to distinguish itself from the atheism and communism of the Soviet Union. The evidence thus suggests that the addition of this motto was a violation of the First Amendment, and so is its common use in government settings.

Of course, every nontheistic organization wants to see the "In God We Trust" motto decommissioned, but the chances of that happening in the foreseeable future aren't very strong. According to AHA Legal Director and Senior Counsel Monica Miller, several courts have ruled that the motto alone, whether on our currency, or on government seals, is constitutional. While we might disagree with the courts' assessments, the chance for a legal victory in such matters simply isn't there. And with the majority of the public and U.S. representatives also supporting the "In God We Trust" motto, building the support for public policy change isn't in view either.

So, when Mississippi changed its standard license plates in 2019 to prominently display "In God We Trust," one might think there was no chance to challenge it. But the facts of the situation are unique. Importantly, if a Mississippian wants an alternative plate, they need to pay extra. And when it comes to license plates, past court rulings have distinguished them from items like currency, saying that there's a higher bar for imposed speech on them. We see this most clearly in a 2019 U.S. District Court ruling in Alabama, *Doe v. Marshall*, which read, in part,

> Currency is not personalized; it says not a word about the person who holds it. Nor is currency displayed; it is exchanged. Hundreds of people may spend the same dollar bill. Identification cards [like license plates], by contrast, are personalized. They are meant to convey substantive personal information about their holders. They are meant to be displayed, never to be given away.

This suggests that a lawsuit that doesn't challenge the motto being on the plate, but rather solely targets the increased cost of the non–"In God We Trust" plate option, would have a stronger chance of success, even in the current cultural and legal climate.

I'm convinced that we should take advantage of chances like the one in Mississippi to make even very small gains. Forcing folks to either advertise their trust in a god or pay extra is obviously wrong, and righting such wrongs is almost always worth it. And winning such a case could set the stage for further victories, continuously narrowing the application of government intrusion into our private views on religious questions. Additionally, the publicity the legal effort receives gives us a chance to educate the public and perhaps sway opinion on the "In God We Trust" motto in general. That's why I'm convinced we shouldn't let the perfect be the enemy of the good and pursue what's pursuable, whenever the odds are in our favor.

Public Policy Outside the Beltway

While this volume focuses mostly on approaches to public policy on the federal level, public policy work on the local and state should not be ignored. A good example of this is found in the Massachusetts Democratic Party's Nontheist Recognition Resolution passed in November 2018. The resolution supports the importance of our growing demographic in political outreach and fights back against the prejudiced idea that atheists and the nonreligious have no moral values. It was drafted by AHA activist Stuart Wamsley with the help of then AHA Legal Director David Niose and introduced by AHA activist Stephen Driscoll.

One challenge as humanist leaders in other states attempt to achieve the same recognition is obtaining the right connections to make such resolutions possible. It was only through Driscoll's sponsorship from within the Democratic Party that the resolution was introduced. These avenues are not open to the general public, but it is not uncommon to find nontheistic delegates and members of these leadership groups. It also helped that Niose and Wamsley had previously represented humanists at the Massachusetts Democratic State Convention, promoting humanist activities and views, so when the time came for a vote, they weren't seen as outsiders.

Another example of local activism is seen in the work of David Williamson, a humanist celebrant and local leader of the Central Florida Freethought Community. When the Brevard County Board of Commissioners voted five to zero to prohibit him from delivering a message to open a board session, he sued them with the help of multiple civil liberties groups. Not only did he win the case, but he also had the opportunity to publicly discuss how humanist invocations are inclusive of everyone, celebrate the diversity of their communities, and acknowledge our common humanity. "Humanistic values are shared by nearly everyone in attendance—whether they admit it or not," Williamson told *Church & State*.

In another instance, when Rhode Island Attorney General Peter Neronha gave the state of Rhode Island's support to the Bladensburg, Maryland Christian cross in the *American Legion v. American Humanist Association* Supreme Court case, local activists went to work. The Humanists of Rhode Island leveraged their connections to friendly organizations to demonstrate to the attorney general that this wasn't an issue solely of concern to atheists. They partnered with the Rhode Island State Council of Churches; Rhode Island Board of Rabbis; American Baptist Churches of Rhode Island; New England Synod, Evangelical Lutheran Church in America; American Civil Liberties Union of Rhode Island; Masjid Al-Islam; Vedanta Society of Providence; National Council of Jewish Women, Rhode Island Action Team; and Rhode Island Conference, United Church of Christ. And it worked! After the coalition pressure was brought to bear, the attorney general withdrew Rhode Island's support of the towering public cross.

Organizing effectively at the local and state levels is essential. As discussed in chapter 10, state constitutions often have provisions making separation of church and state more actionable than in the federal system, and with Republican presidents packing the federal bench with conservatives, the courts are frequently more favorable at the state level. Further, the Religious Right and its allies are very active at the state and local levels. Unless we want to give them uncontested victories, we need to mobilize there as well.

Perhaps the best modern example of Religious Right local organizing is Project Blitz. Journalist David Taylor, writing for the *Guardian*, explained how Christian nationalists are engaged in a legislative assault to reshape America. The Christian right is giving state and local activists a score of "off-the-shelf pro-Christian 'model bills.'" Some of the bills are largely symbolic attempts to publicly imply that the United States is a Christian nation, such as legislation to emblazon "In God We Trust" wherever possible. Others target public schools for infusions of Christianity. And the rest of them seek special rights for religion to discriminate as it sees fit.

Americans United for Separation of Church and State is among those groups leading the charge to expose legislation that would, as the organization's president, Rachel Laser said, "corrupt our cherished principle of separation of religion and government, the cornerstone of religious freedom for all. That's why our broad coalition is joining together to speak out against this divisive, dangerous agenda that has no place in America." A multiyear endeavor, Project Blitz is showing clear signs of further expansion. American Atheists vice president for legal and policy, Alison Gill, reported that over forty new Project Blitz bills were introduced in the first few months of 2019 alone. Clearly our efforts must make room for state and local advocacy.

Going Forward

As AHA Board Member Rob Boston said, speaking to Secular Coalition for America member organizations at a meeting in February 2019, "The Religious Right tells lies with great conviction. We must tell the truth with great conviction." Indeed, we have to rise above what we are now to what we have the potential to become. We have to register our dissent to great wrongs. And most importantly, we must take the reins of public policy advocacy and achieve justice on as broad a scale as possible.

This is a process that benefits from cultivating empathy. Not only does our individual ability to see things from another's perspective help increase our own commitment to compassion, egalitarianism, and justice for all, but it also prevents conflict, because people are less likely to hurt others when they come to understand that we are similar in so many ways. By embracing empathy and overcoming the exceptionalist tendencies of religion and politics, we can realize that we are one people living in this one world—while simultaneously underlining the unfair disadvantages many groups face. Only then can we truly give peace a chance, and thereby give humanity its best chance at survival.

This makes sense in public policy spheres just as much as it does in others. By finding common ground, however narrow, however temporary, we can build the coalitions necessary to accomplish great progress. Locally, we can find ways to ensure services are offered to the needy without unintended harmful side effects. States can clarify that rules that are in place to protect rights and public safety can't be set aside on account of an individual's religious beliefs or other convictions. The federal government can tackle longstanding social justice issues that result in many seeing themselves as second-class citizens today. And on a global scale, the growth of peaceful conflict resolution is something that people of all backgrounds, religious or not, have to encourage if we wish to stop religious and ideological extremists from instigating reprisals both individually and through governments.

Human beings have the potential to reduce violence and promote cooperation on some of the most pressing challenges facing our species. It's time for humanists and allies to bring everything we have to bear on these matters, for failing to do so is equivalent to seeding our future to those who do not grasp who we are, how we got here, or even what true progress for humanity looks like. So let's cultivate our empathy through a humanist lens, where we consciously seek to avoid divisive prejudices—while not erasing differences. Let's create good public policy that affects everyday Americans for the better and creates a culture of egalitarianism. And let's make advancement where and when the opportunity is available to us so we can both move the needle politically and educate folks about humanist perspectives.

Together, we can become a powerful force for making this world a better place.

* * *

Recommended Reading

Greta Christina, *Coming Out Atheist: How to Do It, How to Help Each Other, and Why* (Pitchstone Publishing, 2014).

Marci Hamilton, *God vs. the Gavel: The Perils of Extreme Religious Liberty* (Cambridge, 2014).

Sikivu Hutchinson, *Godless Americana: Race and Religious Rebels* (Infidel Books, 2013).

George Lakoff, *Moral Politics* (University of Chicago Press, 2016).

David Niose, *Fighting Back the Right: Reclaiming America from the Attack on Reason* (St. Martin's Press, 2014).

Richard Rothstein, *The Color of Law* (Liveright Publishing, 2017).

David Suzuki, *The Sacred Balance: Rediscovering Our Place in Nature* (Greystone Books, 2006).

K. Veeramani, *Social Justice: Multiple-Dimensions* (Dravidar Kazhagam, 2013).

ACKNOWLEDGMENTS

* * *

For their personal help with research, editing, ideas, expertise, and advice over the years, I'd like to thank Maggie Ardiente, Jennifer Bardi, Rob Boston, Ken Brooker-Langston, Matthew Bulger, Nicole Carr, Greta Christina, Rachel Deitch, Stephanie Downs Hughes, Fred Edwords, C. Welton Gaddy, Gordon Gamm, Alison Gill, Luis Granados, John Green, Rebecca Hale, Jill Hanauer, Jeff Hawkins, Tony Hileman, John Hooper, Jared Huffman, Sikivu Hutchinson, Jennifer Kalmanson, Woody Kaplan, Sincere Kirabo, Amber Khan, Pritpal Kochhar, jim lampl, Lori Lipman Brown, Ashley Lovelace, Tim Lutero, Sharon McGill, Ron Millar, Monica L. Miller, Monica R. Miller, David Niose, Sunil Panikkath, Anthony Pinn, Rep. Jamie Raskin, Sue Reamer, Paula Rochelle, Melissa Rogers, Leon Seltzer, Ambassador David Saperstein, Scott Seidewitz, Herb Silverman, Mark Smith, Todd Stiefel, Mandisa Thomas, Jason Torpy, Lowell Whitney, John Weinstein, Kristin Wintermute, and Kurt Volkan.

I'd also like to recognize the contributions of those who've come before me and also directly contributed to the thinking that went into this work. Among them are: Janet Jeppson Asimov, Ambassador Carl Coon, Jos Claerbout, Mel Lipman, Anne Mardick, and Sherwin Wine.

ABOUT THE AUTHOR

* * *

Roy Speckhardt has served as executive director of the American Humanist Association since 2005. He is a frequent media commentator who has appeared on *Good Morning America, CNN Headline News, Fox News,* and *National Public Radio,* among others. His articles appear regularly in various publications, including the *Boston Globe, Huffington Post, Patheos,* and the *Humanist.* He has given presentations at universities from Stanford to Oxford, as well as at international gatherings, national conferences, and local humanist-oriented meetings. Speckhardt holds an MBA from George Mason University and a BA in sociology from Mary Washington College. He currently lives and works in Washington, DC.